Writing features

For magazines and websites

Dawn Kennedy

Dedication

To my dear friend Bernard.

Heartfelt thanks for the 021 adventure and an enduring friendship.

CONTENTS

Forward

 Nearly 30 years ago I was a hungry student studying a BA (Honors) in English Literature and Philosophy at Bristol University. I desperately needed some spare cash to support my eating habit. Dutifully, I signed up as a waitress at the local Mexican restaurant and learned to distinguish between enchiladas and tortillas. It was a fine gig as part time jobs went but I spent hours on my feet to earn an amount of money that didn't stretch much further than the next day. My studies were demanding. The turning point came when I was struggling with an essay based on Kant's *Critique of Pure Reason*, a cement block tome of a book that contains not one single attempt at humor. Lost in subtle philosophical arguments, I forgot to go to work.

My next enterprise was to start a woman's magazine, a serious, dreary feminist rag that droned on about the plight of working class women in Birmingham. We sold the magazine on the streets and earned just enough to eat. The magazine's only claim to fame was that it was lampooned in *Private Eye*, a satirical British magazine. Despite bad publicity being better than none, the magazine sank under the weight if its own earnestness.

For a while I worked at Benetton, folding jerseys. Customers, most of whom were potential shoplifters, would come into the store, tear the sweaters of the shelf, and leave me to start the painful process of re-establishing the illusion of perfection. Those who know me will attest that I'm not the colour coded wardrobe kind of girl. More a fling- it -in –and-find- it- when- you-need- it type. Working at Benetton made me swear to never, ever waste a moment of my life ensuring that the corners of my jerseys are kept in line. I lasted a month.

Still hungry, I followed my interest to the local newspaper. I'd always loved newspapers but never considered a career in them - although having opted to study English Literature and Philosophy one would be forgiven for asking if I'd ever considered a career at all. I popped into the offices of the local newspaper, *The Bristol Post*, and asked if they needed someone to make coffee, or maybe write something. My timing was good. A new arts complex had opened at the trendy waterfront and none of the paper's steely eyed, chain smoking newshounds had time to waste watching foreign movies with sub-titles.

And so, at age 19, I got my first writing gig as a film reviewer. I was amazed and delighted that I could get paid to watch and write about movies.

The first film I reviewed was the Japanese classic, *Tampopo*. It tells the story of a truck driver who stops at a small family-run noodle shop and decides to help them perfect their services. It's all about appetite – for food and sex. I thought it was fantastic and wrote 600 lyrical and ecstatic words about the symbolic role of noodles in Japanese film culture.

I took my job very seriously, taking three days to pen my reviews. Every week, between lectures on Kierkegaard and Wordsworth, I'd walk down to the waterfront and sit alone in the dark, scribbling notes about obscure movies. I watched a lot of Japanese movies which oddly always featured an enormous amount of noodles: they seemed to make a guest appearance in nearly every scene, if they didn't play the starring role.

Seeing my name in print gave me immense satisfaction, as did the fact that I earned more money watching and writing about movies than my friends did waiting tables.

But frankly, I had no clue how to write a movie review and wrote by imitating, as best I could, the lofty style of others arts critics.

I continued to write when I settled in Cape Town, mostly book and theatre reviews, features and profiles.

Then I was offered the position as features editor at *O, The Oprah Magazine.*

The opinionated reviews that I was used to writing had no place in Oprah's affirmative feel good world. I found myself without instruction and no clue about the format of first person accounts.

Eventually, I absconded from the world of couch confessional to the dark side, getting a job as the editor of a magazine for smokers. Wielding a lavish budget I sent writers to far flung locations on a whim. I worked in an edgy, politically incorrect environment and had a blast.

Decadence, I'm sad to say, never lasts.

The next ten years saw me working as a freelance writer until, in 2010, I co-launched a startup magazine, *021*. This terrific publication was launched with great optimism and a limited budget at a time when no-one was advertising in magazines. Sad to say, most start-up magazines never last. We published the last issue in December 2013.

The need to eat doesn't abate with age.

I cast my hungry eyes around for my next writing gig. The world had changed. Overnight, it seemed, writers were being paid half the rates for writing. I pitched an 800 word article - *Happiness is a Handbag*, a first person account based on my experience that it's the small things – such as a designer handbag – that make us happy- not the biggies like world peace. The editor commissioned me to write 250 words at R1 per word! Let me put that in perspective. That's less than ten cups of coffee for me to share my philosophical insights with nearly 200 000 readers. No thanks.

Then I got a phone call from the head of the journalism department at a local arts college asking if I'd like to lecture. I come from a long line of teachers – my mother and grandmother were both music teachers. It would be impossible for me to teach in any sort of school setting. But in a college, to students who had paid to learn, to kids who wanted to be journalists...sure!

Stomach growling, I accepted the offer.

Fast forward to me standing in front of 32 wide-eyed journalism students, most of whom are busy texting on their phones. For teaching inspiration I reflected on my experience at Bristol University. There, most lecturers were characters, like the undoubtedly brilliant Polish expert on Sartre who mumbled incomprehensibly (perhaps in Polish) so that nobody could understand a word he said. Andrew Harrison, the aesthetics tutor, helped me form a defensible opinion about art. I'm forever grateful for the hours we spent sipping sherry in his office and discussing the fine line between art and pornography.

The sherry wasn't an option in my lectures, but taking my cue from Andrew's freewheeling conversationalist style, I chatted amiably to my class about the challenges and pleasures of writing features.

They looked at me blankly. The soulful, winding and profound route to education was not what these generation Y students wanted. They wanted power points and step by step instruction. Not wanting to disappoint them, or fail at the teaching task, I attempted to teach features in a clear bullet point fashion – complete with power points and YouTube videos.

Although there is no precise formula for writing a feature, there are certain tips and signposts that can make the undoubtedly difficult task easier.

Nothing in this book is original. As I struggled to learn to teach features I relied on instruction through books. I read everything on writing features that I could get my hands on. I found something of value in nearly every book and would encourage you to read as widely as possible. Two books, in particular, helped me immensely: William Zinsser's *On Writing Well* and *Telling True Stories* by Mark Kramer and Wendy Call. Serious students of writing should rush out immediately and buy these books. I quote liberally from them as they offer expert advice from the world's best practitioners.

I now believe that features can be taught (if students are willing to learn).

I've used my own examples throughout this book examples from outstanding writers, such as Gay Talese and Truman Capote. I do this with humility. Examples from masters of the craft are intended to give you something to reach for. I liberally use my own samples for a practical reason: They offer no problems with plagiarism or copyright and make this book more personal and original.

One thing I know for sure is that I love writing and reading features. My sincere hope is that this book will inspire you and offer sufficient instruction to help you write the stories you long to tell and I long to read.

CHAPTER 1: GETTING STARTED

Who is this book for?

I've written *Writing Features* to help absolutely anyone who has an interest in writing feature articles, either for magazines, newspapers, or the internet. Below are a few groups of people that I think might specifically benefit from this book:

Journalism students

Many journalism courses barely mention writing features, even though most hard news publications include regular features. The ability to write features should be part of any journalist's repertoire. Writing features is rewarding, enabling you to go deeper into a story and forcing you to expand your literary ability. It also keeps your passion alive. Writing formulaic news stories day after day can become draining. It's inspiring for Journalists to be working on a feature that they care about, or enjoy, as well as writing news.

Bloggers

If you write a regular blog, knowing how to write features will help you create quality content fast and make the most use of the content that you have. The same material can be worked into a list feature, a how-to feature, and an interview. Learning how to use the different feature formats for your blog will keep your content varied and lively, catering for a diversity of readers. Taking time to study this book will give your blogging a professional, authoritative feel that will help you attract and keep readers.

Experts and enthusiasts

Do you have an interest? A hobby? Whatever it is, from tea drinking, to Metallica music, I guarantee that there's a website or publication dedicated to fans. Why not write features about your hobby? It will keep you in contact with other enthusiasts, encourage you to develop your expertise and possibly contribute towards funding your hobby.

Travellers

There is a whole writing industry related to travel. If you have a career in travel, say as a tour guide, writing travel features can provide an outlet for your expertise and earn you extra income. If you love travel, writing travel features can get you free hotel accommodation and even flight tickets. Writing about travel will make you a better traveller. It will encourage you to get off the beaten track, speak to local people and look at the places you visit with clearer eyes.

Stay at home parents

Being at home with babies and young children can be both rewarding and frustrating. If you are a stay at home mum or dad, it's guaranteed that you can write from an interesting angle for a parenting themed magazine – one of the largest magazine segments. Writing features when you are at home, thanks to the internet, is both possible and lucrative.

Young adults

Magazines love youth and are always looking for young talent. Think about turning your experiences into features. First person accounts are a great place for young people to start. My son fulfilled his desire to skydive and paraglide by writing articles about the experiences.

Students

As a student you are in touch with issues that are arising in your field. For example, as a medical student, you could write a first person report on what it's like to work the gruelling hours that your internship requires. As someone who is in a learning position you are ideally placed to explain issues to the general public about your field. For example, as a computer scientist, you could write an article on the future of apps using your professors as sources.

Golden agers

The two most essential ingredients for writers are curiosity and time. Keeping curious is the best way to keep young and writing actually cultivates curiosity – knowing that you have to write about something invites you to take a closer look at it and inevitably the more involved you become with anything the more interesting it reveals itself to be. When you are retired, you have the time necessary to pursue and write stories.

Established writers

Writing is a difficult craft and every writer needs occasional doses of inspiration and instruction. While this book is written for the beginner, writers at every stage of their career can hopefully find something useful.

Freelance writers

While not addressing the issue of how to build a freelance career, this book will teach you how to expand your repertoire and boost your income through writing different types of features.

"Thank God for stories – for those who have them, for those who tell them, for those who devour them as the soul sustenance that they are. Stories give shape to experience and allow us to go through life unblind. Without them, everything that happens would float around, undifferentiated. None of it would mean anything. Once you have a version of what happened all the other good stuff about being human comes into play. You can laugh, feel awe, commit a passionate act, get pissed, want to change things."

Alex Tizon quoted by Jacqui Banaszynski in *Telling True Stories*

Why write features?

Quite honestly, there's absolutely no reason why you should write features and not do something more practical, like beekeeping or dentistry. Announcing to your family that you want to write for a living is likely to be met with furrowed brows.

Most people don't set out in life wanting to write features. I stumbled into it, as many others do, when I discovered the doors to employment for English and philosophy graduates were not exactly wide open.

Five things I wish I'd known about writing features when I was younger:

1.   Five things I wish I'd known about … is a great formula for writing features – Five things I wish I'd known about having kids, Five things I wish I'd known when I studied philosophy, Five things I wish I'd known when I was twenty. Argh. Stop me already.

2.   I wish that I'd known what I was doing when I was writing features. Especially about ledes. I read over my work now and some of my features beg for a good anecdotal lede. When I think of the lonely hours spent at

my desk agonizing over how to start a story while all the time there were tricks and tools that could have made my task easier.

3.   I wish I'd had more instruction. A mentor, a William Zinsser kind of guy, who would have leaned over my shoulder, making kindly suggestions, such as, "Maybe you should try a scenic lede here." In the absence of this, I learned through imitation – a haphazard approach. There was always a nagging sense of "Am I doing this right?" In retrospect I could have written many of my features better had I known what is set forth in this book.

4.   I wish I'd known how to earn more money from writing. I wish I'd known how to recycle my articles. This has nothing to do with putting them on the compost heap, but rather reworking material into different feature formats. I was so passionate about writing that I spent ages writing articles, taking my eye off the money and not using my material to its full extent. I wish I'd known how one interview could result in a Q&A for one publication, a profile for another and become the basis of a general feature for a third.

5.   I wish I'd stood by my work more. I never really felt that I had a career as a writer. Sitting typing in my pyjamas felt somehow slovenly. Now that I am a teacher and change out of my pyjamas at 6am, there's a sense of societal approval. And yet, I worked harder as a writer than I did in any other job. It was 24/7, seven days a week. I was either thinking of an idea for a story, pitching a story, or writing a story.

Despite the above mild regrets, I'm absolutely delighted to have spent the majority of my life writing.

Here's why

1.   I have a treasure trove of memories. Some people have their photographs, I have features stories. Each article has a date and a by-line, reminding me where I was and what I was doing at that particular time.

2.   I'm well connected. I have met some wonderful people. Being an immigrant writer is a wonderful thing. In Cape Town, my adopted city, I know many people from many different walks of life.

3.   I've had great experiences. I have a low boredom threshold and I'm not good sitting around idly. One of the beauties of being a writer is that I can turn family vacations into an article.

4.   I've scored wonderful freebies. I've never calculated how much I've earned through writing, which is probably a good thing. However, writing has earned me an incalculable amount of freebies: books galore, beauty treatments, and weekends at guest houses and meals at top restaurants.

5.   I've avoided the 9-5. As a writer I was freer to come and go than most and worked smarter and harder. What is the point in wasting an hour in traffic to get somewhere by 9am when you can schedule an interview for 10am and get two hours writing in before breakfast? None, I say.

6.   I've kept interested in life. I'm constantly amazed by just how fascinating life is. Writing has not only allowed me to indulge my curiosity, but it's helped develop it. Like everyone, there are times that I feel jaded. Then along comes a writing assignment that makes me realize that I've just been nibbling the edge of the cookie of life and that the delicious melting part in the middle still remains. Through writing I've developed an interest in opera and bird watching. Two hobbies I never could have imagined I would enjoy.

7.   I've kept fit. As someone who wrote about trends I got to try out every fitness fad on the block, from hot yoga to boot camp. Writing features, unlike writing fiction, gets you out into the world and keeps you active.

"If you want to be a writer, you must do two things above all others: read a lot and write a lot."

Stephen King

Preparation: Read and write voraciously

In *Outliers: The Story of Success*, Malcolm Gladwell outlines the 10,000-Hour Rule, claiming that the key to success in any field is, to a large extent, a matter of practicing a specific task for a total of around 10,000 hours. This, combined with Stephen King's advice, means that if you want to write features you have to do two things: read voraciously and write voraciously. It doesn't actually matter how well you do these things, by simply reading and writing on a daily basis your writing will get better.

The Clippings File

As you work through the first section of this book, you will be creating a clippings file. This project serves four purposes.

Firstly, it encourages you to read widely, from a variety of sources. The rule for compiling your clippings file is that each it should contain only one article from any publication per genre.

Secondly, it familiarizes you with the layout of magazines, e-zines and websites.

Thirdly, it gives you a clear visual representation of the different types of features and reminds you of their structure.

Finally, once you are pitching and writing articles it gives you good examples to follow. One of the best ways to learn a skill is to copy others who have mastered it.

What you need:

A file

Plastic sheeting

A cache of magazines

Access to the internet

Instructions

At the end of each sub-section of the chapter, Types of Features, you will be instructed to spend a week reading each type of feature and choosing three examples from either print or online to add to your file.

"The hard news story marches briskly through the what's, when's, where's, looking neither left nor right, packing in enough details to give readers a clear picture.

In features, the immediacy of the event is secondary. The plain ladder of descending news values is replaced by human interest, mood, atmosphere, emotion, irony, humour. Features aim to give readers' pleasure and entertainment along with...information"

Rene J. Cappon, editor of the Associated Press

What is a Feature?

There is no common agreement about what constitutes a feature. A feature is everything that is not hard news, which editors of newspapers, magazines and websites commission and journalists and bloggers write. This includes: Information features; interview features; profiles; human interest stories; background stories; travel features; reviews and narrative features. It also includes investigative features which require skills that are beyond the scope of this book.

Many journalists will argue that an interview, with its simple Q&A format, lacks sufficient writing skill to be a feature. However, the Q&A makes a regular appearance in newspapers and is a staple of almost every magazine. I've no intention of offending the thirteenth feature fairy and not including the Q&A in a definition of features.

Hence, I define features as:

Content that regularly appears in media, both print and online, which includes some news values and which is designed to educate, inform or entertain.

This definition is broad and sweeping enough to include both information features and columns.

My reasons for opting for such a generalized definition of features is that novice writers will be expected to write any of the features included in this book. While your aim may be to write narrative features, the likelihood is that an editor will first commission you to submit a less demanding story first, such as a Q&A or information feature.

Knowing about the different types of features will help you pitch professional query letters and equip you to fulfil any writing assignment that comes your way.

Another reason for approaching features in this way is that if you want to work as a freelance feature writer, in order to earn a living you will need to repackage your stories and sell them in different formats to several publications. For example, an interview with the Minister for Education could be an interview feature, a list feature (My five favourite educational websites), a profile or the basis for a general feature on, for example, the poor literacy levels among school leavers.

Finally, if you have aspirations to work on a magazine, you need to know not just how to write, but how magazines work.

HOW MAGAZINES WORK

Most magazine readers know that their favourite publication has a similar look and feel each month and appreciate its familiarity. Yet few outside the industry realize how strictly a magazine is formatted. Each magazine has a template, known as a flat plan, and each day, week, or month, writers are commissioned by editors to write content and features according to that flat plan.

This is vital to grasp. As a writer you don't get to call up an editor and say, "Hey, I've got this great idea for a story on Inner City graffiti, how about it? " Writing for magazines is a well-choreographed dance. The good news is that if you know the moves you can impress editors and keep your fingers flying across the keyboard. But, as with any new endeavour, you need to take time to learn the conventions of the dance or you will step on toes.

What feature writers need

Writing features is a process. Writing is in many ways the easy part.

A good feature writer requires four essential skills.

1.   An ability to come up with good story idea

2.   An ability to sell a story to an editor

3.   An ability to research a story

4.   An ability to write well.

With the combination of diverse skills needed to write features, it's no wonder that becoming a successful feature writer is a tough proposition.

You will notice that I've put the ability to sell a story before the ability to write a story. This is not an error. If you can't sell the story, there's no point in spending time researching and writing it. Unless, of course, you have a nice trust fund and can afford to wander around indulging your whims. In which case, drop me a mail – I've got some great projects that need financing.

HOW ARE FEATURES WRITTEN?

Each category of feature has its own conventions, discussed in separate chapters.

Certain features, such as the Q&A and basic information features, are formulaic and require a minimum of research and writing skills. However, within their limited framework, they offer the opportunity to shine. So don't dismiss these types of features as unworthy of attention. They are staples in nearly every magazine, so there are plenty of opportunities to write them. Although these features require less skill to write, they enable you to add content quickly to your website and put food on the table.

Profiles, human interest stories and general features demand more reporting and writing skill. They use literary devices, such as vivid description, dialogue and conflict to build character and drive a compelling narrative.

A first person account requires less reporting but a confident writing style and a distinct voice.

Columns require no reporting but a flair for amusing readers and holding their interest.

When you are starting out as a feature writer knowing the different genres of features allows you to explore different mediums and find your strengths. For ages, I was pigeon holed as a reviewer, simply because that's how I started out. It took me a long time to practice writing other types of feature and discover that I loved writing profiles and first person accounts. I've also learned that my interest shifts. Right now I'm ready to do some deep reporting on a significant social issue. Knowing the different types of features that you can write helps you vary the type of writing that you do which will keep you energized and interested in your craft.

News values

All journalists are trained to recognize what are called news values which evaluate potential stories in relation to their readers. News values decide what stories are written and how much space and prominence they are given in the media. News values also apply to features, although to a lesser degree.

Eight commonly identified news values are:

Impact

Relevance

Proximity

Prominence

Timeliness

Conflict

Currency

The unusual.

Feature writers and news reporters often write about the same topic, but approach it in different ways.

Below are listed ways in which feature writers adapt news values for their stories:

Impact and Relevance:

In feature writing, these two news values are often entwined. What has an impact on our lives is relevant and we want to know more about it. Features are often adept at unpacking the impact and relevance of news for readers. In fact, one convention of feature writing – the nut graf– is a short paragraph that tells readers why they should care about a particular issue. For example, why should we care about frakking? What relevance does it have in our lives?

Proximity:

Issues that happen regularly in our cities and countries are often given short shrift in the newspapers. For example, rape is an everyday occurrence in South Africa. But the journalist who writes a human interest story on the impact of one particular rape can highlight the issue more than yet another news flash. Author Charlene Smith drives home the proximity of rape with an account beginning with this powerful lede: "Every 26 seconds in South Africa a woman gets raped. It was my turn last Thursday night."

Prominence:

Many features, whether interview pieces or profiles, are about famous people. While many people feel that famous people get undue attention in the press, the prominent are still food for features. Try to feature people who are prominent in interesting ways i.e. – famous for more than their chiselled cheekbones and physical attributes.

Timeliness:

Magazines and websites will interview actors before the release of a new film. It can be argued that this is more of a publicity value than a news value, but timeliness also applies to more in-depth features. On the other hand, well written features can ignore timeliness altogether. For example, Patricia Marx's first person account, published in the New Yorker of driving in LA, is a timeless article - New Yorkers are perennially interested in comparing their lifestyle to the inhabitants of Los Angeles.

Conflict:

Conflict, antagonism and tension are the stuff of feature stories. Wherever you find conflict, or two people with antagonistic opinions, you have the stuff of human drama and a potentially good feature.

Currency:

When a news event gains currency, readers clamour for features about the issue. South Africans' experienced this with the high profile Oscar Pistorius trial. As well as round the clock coverage of every word spoken, barrels of ink were spilt on the issues surrounding the trial: features about disability, male violence, the Afrikaner laager mentality, crime in South Africa, gun laws and the link between aggression and competitive sports have all gained media space by association with the trial.

The unusual:

In the nineteenth century John B. Bogarg of the New York Sun gave a catchy definition of news: "It's not news if a dog bites a man, but if a man bites a dog, then it's news." Many features are of the man bites dog persuasion. Human interest features often report on people who display unusual courage or who are eccentric in a fascinating way.

Chapter 2: Types of features

The interview feature

Get people talking. Learn to ask questions that will elicit answers about what is most interesting in their lives. Nothing so animates writing as someone telling what he thinks or what he does – in his own words.

His own words will always be better than your words, even if you are the most elegant stylist in the land. They carry the inflection of his speaking voice and the idiosyncrasies of how he puts a sentence together. They contain the regionalisms of his conversation and the lingo of his trade. They convey his enthusiasms. This is a person talking to the reader directly, not through the filter of a writer. As soon as a writer steps in, everyone else's experience become second-hand."

William Zinsser *On Writing Well*

The Q&A

The most basic form of the interview feature is the straightforward question and answer format, or Q&A, which as its name suggests is questions posed by the journalist, followed by their answers. This allows a reader to "hear" the actual words by the celebrity. Take, for example, this Q& A with Don Cheadle in GQ by Mary Kaye Schilling: Cheadle is quoted as saying, "Yeah – look, I can be as neurotic as the next person. I'm not cavalier. I get nervous about my career too. But I feel like what's supposed to happen is going to happen." The effect is that the reader feels like they are overhearing a spontaneous, unscripted conversation. Of course, that's an illusion as the celebrity is choosing his or her words carefully and the writer is editing scrupulously.

The Q&A is often derided as unworthy of journalist's time. However, Bill Kovach and Tom Rosenstielin in *The Elements of Journalism* quote Jay Rosen, a New York University journalism professor at a journalism conference as saying that he considers the Q&A form to be a powerful but underused method: "It forces the journalist to frame the material around things that citizens might ask. It also allows audiences to scan a story and enter it wherever they want, rather than having to read it from the top down. Interestingly, this has become a favoured form on websites in the form of frequently asked questions (FAQ's)".

The interview feature

One of the best proponents of the probing interview piece is English journalist Lynn Barber. Her interviews were not respectful transcripts, but as Rachel Cooke, writing about her in *The Observer* describes, "Mesmerizing encounters in which, like a wrestler, she was wont to fling her subjects against the ropes – older hacks would warn her about objectivity. Thankfully, she ignored them. Like any good writer, she is entirely on the side of the reader, who expects and deserves to be entertained."

Before dismissing the interview feature as entertaining fluff, consider Oriana Fallaci's incisive interviews with dictators and politicians and interrogations of leaders such as Kissinger and Qaddafi in Interview with History.

In a tribute to Fallaci, published in Vanity Fair, Christopher Hitchens demonstrates the subtle power of asking questions in the right way.

He derides an excerpt from a bumbling interview "with what our media culture calls a 'world leader'."

Dan Rather: Mr. President, I hope you will take this question in the spirit in which it's asked. First of all, I regret that I do not speak Arabic. Do you speak any ... any English at all?

Saddam Hussein: (through translator): Have some coffee.

Rather: I have coffee.

Hussein: (through translator): Americans like coffee.

Rather: That's true. And this American likes coffee.

Hitchens compares this inane interchange with Fallaci's incisive interview with another "world leader."

Fallaci: When I try to talk about you, here in Tehran, people lock themselves in a fearful silence. They don't even dare pronounce your name, Majesty. Why is that?

The Shah: Out of an excess of respect, I suppose.

Fallaci: I'd like to ask you: if I were an Iranian instead of an Italian, and lived here and thought as I do and wrote as I do, I mean if I were to criticize you, would you throw me in jail?

The Shah: Probably.

As Hitchens writes, "With Oriana Fallaci's demise at 77 from a host of cancers, in September, in her beloved Florence, there also died something of the art of the interview."

SAMPLE: Here's the start of a Basic Q&A:

Dawn Kennedy meets Mark Forsyth, the author of the witty, ribald Sunday Times number one bestseller *The Etymologicon: A Circular Stroll Through the Hidden Connections of the English Language.*

Q: When did your interest in the connections between words begin?

A: I was given a copy of the Oxford English Dictionary as a christening present and I've never really recovered.

Q: Is your aim to entertain or educate?

A: My plan was to write a book to be read on the lavatory. My highest literary aim was to give the world slightly more informative and entertaining emunctions. So I wanted to make people laugh, but not too hard.

Q: Just how intertwined is language?

A: It's everywhere, but you just don't notice unless you stop and think. So awful (meaning bad) and awesome (meaning good) are quite obviously from the same root, but you'd never notice. You go further back and find that video and wisdom and the Sanskrit Vedas all come from the same root, which meant to see and understand.

Etc.,

More complex interview features weave more of the writer's observations and paraphrasing into the feature.

SAMPLE: Below is an excerpt from an example of an interview feature that I wrote about a famous South African comedian, Pieter-Dirk Uys:

Armed only with a suitcase full of costumes, a sense of outrage and pages of witty words against society's ills, Pieter Dirk Uys has gifted South Africa with laughter that has lightened even the darkest times. "Being funny about things that aren't funny, being successful entertaining huge paying audiences with stories no one wants to hear: that's my show business," declares Pieter Dirk Uys.

I first interviewed Pieter six years ago, making the pilgrimage to Darling to touch the hem of the great humourist. Along the N7 to Malmesbury, the sky opens like a yawn and I feel myself shake off the stress of Cape Town and slide into a more relaxed small town South African pace.

Inside the darkened space of Evita Se Peron, the train station that Peter converted into a theatre, the Afrikaans memorabilia that crams the walls is cloying. While waiting for Pieter, I'm reminded of reluctant visits to the mouldy homes of old relatives.

What ensued was not so much an interview as a graceful onslaught of verbal dexterity. Pieter slipped in and out of character, becoming Evita Bezuidenhout and Pik Botha, by turns, giving me the impression that he uses any conversation as an opportunity to practice timing. He didn't chat; he delivered speech, peppered with idioms that have slid into South African vernacular. For two hours he held my attention in the palm of his hand with a sweeping intelligence which embraced politics, people and history.

In the tradition of Shakespeare's fools, he summed up the state of play in society with catchy phrases like, "Love your enemy, it will ruin their reputation" and "I put the mock in democracy."

George Bernard Shaw famously said "if you want to tell people the truth you'd better make them laugh, or they'll kill you." Naturally Pieter has coined his own version of the quote: "Most of the things I say are not jokes. They are the truth. But the truth can be very funny."

Pieter swears by what he calls a "magical definition: "49 per cent anger versus 51 per cent entertainment has always been a good guide for me through the thirty years of staying on top of my profession."

Continues...

Ends...

When I think of Pieter Dirk Uys, I don't find any visual image coming into focus. Maybe that's because he is protean by nature. Or maybe it's because he's so identified with his work that the mask and the man have become inseparable. I'm left with a sound, the sound of laughter: titters, guffaw, howls and gales of laughter follow him wherever he goes. But mostly it's Archbishop Desmond Tutu's inimitable giggle that sticks in my mind. Desmond Tutu takes unashamed delight in watching himself being mimicked by Peter. When Peter jokes that he loves Tutu because at least there's one other guy in South Africa wearing a dress, Tutu starts up a rhythmical teeheeeheehe that lasts about five minutes and sounds like manna from heaven.

TASK. Spend the week immersed in reading interviews.

Read these three classics:

1.   Oriana Fallaci interviewing the Ayatollah Khomeini in Interviews with History

2.   Truman Capote, The Duke in his Domain, the New Yorker

3.   Lynn Barber interviewing Christopher Hitchens in the Guardian

Clippings file

Collect 3 interview features of varying lengths and complexity, from 800 words up to 5, 000 words. When you have selected your three favourites, print them and add them to your clippings file.

The Profile

At its best, the celebrity profile fosters a feeling of warm intimacy. We read the profile and we feel that we have been granted access not just to the contents of the celebrity's overnight bag but to the contents of his or her heart. Yet this same profile simultaneously manages to reveal no new information. We love it because it confirms our best beliefs. No other form so seamlessly constructs the necessary components of celebrity, exploiting our desire to see our idol as both 'just like us' and nothing like us, as both the girl next door and a goddess above. It is, in other words, spectacularly banal.

Anne Helen Peterson, *The Banality of the Celebrity Profile.*

One of the most popular types of features, profiles are feature stories about either celebrated or ordinary people. Profiles bring people to life and make readers believe they are getting an intimate peek at their entire lives, not just a single conversation.

Profiles enlarge on the interview, adding the writer's psychological insight and including the perceptions of others.

A profile is not a biography. A biography is an account of a person's life, either comprehensive and chronological, or limited to significant milestones and accomplishments. Profile features keep biographical information in the background, weaving it into the author's observations about the subject. Profiles aim to answer the question, "What makes this person tick?"

Celebrity profiles

As novice journalists, chances are that you won't be given celebrity profiles to write. That's not a bad thing. As Jane Kramer says in *The New, New Journalism* "I've deliberately avoided writing about people you would call celebrities because they leave me no freedom as a writer. There is nothing to create from. Because somebody famous is already, by definition, a finished product."

So never mind that you won't get to lunch with Joaquin Phoenix, writing profiles about relatively unknown people in your community will give you freedom.

Profiles about places

While profiles are usually in-depth portraits of people, occasionally the portrait is of a place, for example, *Crossing Over*, J.R Moehringer's portrait of Gee's Bend described how a proposed ferry to the mainland might impact the isolated river community in Alabama, mostly populated by descendants of slaves.

SAMPLE: Here's an excerpt from a profile that I wrote about Maitland Cemetery in Cape Town.

In Maitland Cemetery, where passion entwines with mortality, a team of committed workers ensure that the dead are given a dignified exit.

At the mandala-like centre of Cape Town's 100 hectare cemetery, two workers scrape their brooms calmly through the dust, making a cicada-like noise that sounds like a teacher telling students to "shush". But for the dead who lie in Maitland cemetery, it's too late to learn any more lessons.

Here, the brief and brutal lives of Cape Town's gangsters are etched onto the tombstones and the sound of gunshots accompanies them into eternity. James Thomas, who has worked for 26 years as a tombstone layer, says, "Gangsters are our main customers. They have a short life. If they die, the boss looks after them." And, if they're the boss? Then, having spent a life of skullduggery, they will be laid to rest in a splendid structure, replete with pillars. Lording over the cemetery is the resting place of the notorious gang leader Coleen Stanfield. "His grave cost R74 000," says James, "and a lot of trouble." On the day he was buried, police lined the perimeter of the cemetery, rifles cocked towards the graveside, ready to step in and stop the violence if rival gangs appeared.

The undertakers are a jovial bunch. It seems that being close to death reminds them to enjoy their allotted lifespan: pot bellies, deep laughter and smile wrinkled faces are evident among them.

Throughout the day, the tombstone layers troop in and out of the record office, a grim place that the electronic age hasn't yet reached. Everybody buried at Maitland cemetery, dating back to the first burial on 16 January 1886, is recorded as a hand-written entry in a dusty ledger. The books are almost disintegrating, their pages threadbare and torn, but the tombstone layers flick through them as though looking for a number in a telephone directory, double-checking that their tombstones are allocated to the correct grave, regardless of the fact that tearing a page might eradicate evidence of a corpse's resting place forever.

1994 brought big changes to the business of burial. Until then, three institutions monopolized the death market: Cliff, Gardener and Monumental Art. But after 1994, new laws opened up the market and soon entrepreneurs like Ronnie Abernaud began offering tombstones at a quarter of the price. However, this new freedom has brought a scourge of opportunism. "The bakkie gang," as James calls them, have been making a quick profit, passing off cheap concrete tombstones as genuine granite, designed to weather all elements into eternity. Unwitting mourners, who spend up to R10 000 for a granite tombstone, are dismayed to find that in less than a year, concrete starts to poke through the spray-painted granite effect and the writing on the tombstone begins to vanish.

Cond., read full article @ www.dawnkennedywriter.com

Profiles about sub-cultures

Occasionally what is profiled is neither a person nor a place but a sub-culture. Here's an excerpt from a profile that I wrote about the scene around 2oceansvibe, a popular Cape Town blog:

They're alive and clicking – Cape Town's cyber-tribes – online communities bonded by shared interests and values. At the forefront of this trend is 2oceansvibe.com, one of Cape Town's most popular websites. 021 slung on some high heels and went to explore a world where the Veuve Clicquot is always on ice and the vibe is all that matters.

One simple word – vibe – defines the 2oceansvibe tribe. According to their ethos, everything – people, parties, brands – has a vibe, and the author of the website, self-styled, commitment phobic playboy Seth Rotherham, has made it his vocation to declare who, what, and where has the right vibe i.e. the vibe he likes.

His readers and fans are not complex people. They want the good life – the babes, the cars, the cocktails. But most of all, they want an intangible, indefinable something, namely the vibe. 2oceansvibe people are fresh young things, upwardly mobile and socially gifted, or affluent over-30-year-olds, compensating for youth with good dental work and a sense of style.

2oceansvibe proclaims: "Work is a sideline. Live the holiday." If you edge towards angst, and prefer gazing at your navel than your reflection in the mirror, you're not likely to get the vibe. If you are plagued by a Protestant work ethic, or prefer the security of 9–5 to the freedom of freelancing, you're not part of the vibe. If you object to women going topless, are weighed down by social concerns, or generally approach life with a furrowed brow, you don't belong in this group. Clearly that doesn't exclude too many people: The pages of 2oceansvibe.com are visited more than 50 000 times per month. The South African blog awards gave 2oceansvibe the following accolades: Best Overall Blog; Best Entertainment Blog; Most Humorous Blog; Best Post; Best Original Writing; Most Controversial Blog. Fans and readers love the intoxicated flow of consciousness commentary penned by Seth.

Like every tribe, it has its sub-cultures. Hanging out in the base chakra are the okes, generally thick necked beer drinkers who just want to ogle the topless girls in provocative poses who decorate the site. Part of Seth's job description is the daunting task of selecting compromising pictures of naked celebrities to post on his site. Mention Seth's name to some and you will get the response 'sexist pig'. Among others, there's the perception that 2oceansvibe is some kind of privileged boys-only club. One crestfallen girl said, "I'd love to be part of the tribe, but it's more of a guy thing."

Then there are the material boys and girls who look like they've stepped out of a Peter Stuyvesant ad. These are Cape Town's high class, well-heeled hedonists who pride themselves on knowing where and how to have a good time. They live for the moment, don't take life too seriously, and can party like there's no tomorrow. Fuelled by copious quantities of Double Olmeca Black tequila and Pussy energy drink mix, these are the people who will, at some stage of inebriation, dance on the bar, or reveal their mammary glands in public.

A cyber-tribe is invisible, but this one regularly materializes for the Sunday night shakedown at Caprice. While the rest of the world is winding down, preparing for the week ahead, they flaunt their freedom, draining the last drop of fun from the weekend. Going against the grain like this speaks to Seth's soul. It was here, in 2002, that the concept of 2oceansvibe was born. Seth reveals, "We were having so much fun I wanted to share the vibe with others."

Read full article: www.dawnkennedywriter.com

SAMPLE: profile about a person: Here's an extract from a profile that I wrote about a local health enthusiast:

Dawn Kennedy gets on the same wavelength as Cape Town ecopreneur Joseph Feigelson.

Joseph Feigelson is passionate about sprouts and eats nearly three hands full a day. It's no wonder; 13 years ago they cured his debilitating heartburn. The alternative was acid reflux surgery, a rather unpleasant procedure. Since incorporating sprouts into his diet, Joseph has abundant energy and hasn't spent a single day sick in bed.

As well as giving him back his health, sprouts have been sustaining Joseph financially and he has feathered his nest in the most novel way – with a home sprouting kit called Kitchen Garden. It's ingenious in its incredible simplicity: a cardboard box containing six jam jars, some gauze, elastic bands, six packets of seed, a metal structure and a tray – everything you need to grow sprouts in the comfort of your kitchen – and it's yours for R400. Within three days, having rinsed your seeds twice daily and allowed them to drip-dry on the tray, you will have an abundance of edible sprouts; your very own garden in a jam jar.

The magic of sprouts is that they are rich in enzymes and that, unlike vegetables that start losing their nutritional value the moment they are harvested, sprouts are still growing as we eat them and practically buzzing with vitamins and minerals.

....

Somehow the conversation takes a detour and we talk about cloud-busting. How we got onto the topic is a mystery. It's like that with Joseph. He's a matrix of information. Poised between a flat-screen television emitting a low volume stream of misery about an oil spill in the Mexican Gulf and a computer that draws his attention compulsively, I'm struck, as always, by people's glorious contradictions. Shouldn't Joseph be living Robinson Crusoe-style in a beach hut rather than in suburbia? Shouldn't he be watching grass grow rather than satellite television? The conversation takes another 180 degree turn back to food, this time nuts, and I'm on safer, more solid ground.

Joseph tells me about the time he was flying business class with his wealthy ex-wife and found himself seated next to the tycoon Ed Azar, owner of the second largest nut company in the world. With characteristic forthrightness Joseph asked him: "Why do you put so much crap on your nuts?" Azar replied: "Hell, I really don't know but I'll pay you to find out." Three months later, Joseph, by now divorced, was knocking on Azur's door to see if his offer still held good. It did. The tycoon paid him generously to spend several months researching the potential market for organic nuts in the United States.

What Joseph discovered was that the list of chemicals as long as your arm in commercial nuts could be attributed to one thing: salt. "You must know what a scary thing salt is," he tells me. Joseph watched the production of salted peanuts and was appalled to discover that vats of salt were bleached to disguise rat droppings and packed with anticaking agent and aluminium oxide to make it run from the container like powdered sand.

Joseph advised Azur to remove the salt and sell his nuts dry roasted, natural and organic. He lets me sample his unquestionably delicious dry-roasted nut mixture, joking, "As they say, you are what you eat. I'm nuts."

Read full article @ www.dawnkennedywriter.com

TASK: Spend the week immersed in reading profile features.

Read these three classics:

1.   Frank Sinatra Has a Cold, by Gay Talese, *Esquire*, 1966

2.   The Peekaboo Paradox, by Gene Weingarten, *the Washington Post*

3.   Crossing Over J.R Moehringer's portrait of Gee's Bend,

Collect 3 profile features of varying lengths and complexity, from 800 words up to 5, 000 words. When you have selected your three favourites, print them and add them to your clippings file.

The human interest story

"The feature writer's aim is the dramatists aim: make 'em laugh; make 'em weep."

Mary J.J. Rimm *The Elements of Journalism*

The human interest feature reflects our interest in each other. Designed to make readers feel, it presents people and their problems, concerns, or achievements in a way that evokes empathy in the reader. Reading human interest stories makes us think, "Oh, the humanity."

The range of human interest stories is endless. However several types of stories occur regularly:

Acts of courage: Readers love stories about ordinary people being brave and heroic, such as the story of the two teenagers who chased a carjacker and saved two kids ages two and six.

Triumph over adversity: Reader's relish stories about people winning against the odds, beating cancer, battling back from bankruptcy or surviving a mugging.

Anniversaries: Readers are interested in finding out how people are coping after either tragedy or unexpected good fortune. For example, one year after a divorce or one year after winning the lottery are both popular features. A good reporter will enter story ideas in her diary 12 months ahead.

Compassionate people. Next to courage, readers are interested in kindness: Glen, who had been living on the streets of Boston, found a backpack stuffed with $42,000 that he decided to turn over to police so it could be reunited with its owner. You want to read on and find out more, right? Or how about the story of hundreds of strangers turning up at the funeral of a World War 2 veteran who died with no close family or friends.

Major achievements: Amidst all the bad news in the papers, readers enjoy celebrating those who have battled and succeeded. For example, the dyslexic boy who has just passed his proofreading exams, or the woman with a terrible fear of flying who has just become an air hostess.

People and their pets: People love stories about the special bond between humans and their pets. For example, the dog who leads his owner to discover an elderly man freezing in snow, or the dolphins who rescue a surfer from a shark attack, or the cat who walked 70 miles to find his old home when the family moved.

Reunions: It's amazing to read about people who meet up after long separations. For example, the story of the Indian boy who lost his mother in 1986 and found her 25 years later by using Google Earth. Or, the man who decided to look for his biological mother and discovered she was the bearded woman. If that's not strange enough, how about the long-lost brothers who discovered they were neighbours?

Eccentrics: what would the world be without eccentrics? For example, the man who invented a device that straightens bananas, or the man who crossed the English Channel in a bath tub to get into the Guinness Book of Records.

Victims: These are the "weepy" tales of real sadness: the mum who lost her baby twins to cot death; the young couple who got married in hospital two days before the bride died of cancer or the parents who have left their children to die in the backseat of a vehicle.

Unsung heroes: The 83-year-old who has served dinners at a day centre for 20 years because he likes to do his bit for the "old folk."

Many human interest stories are not so easily categorized.

SAMPLE: Below is a story that I wrote about children in the township learning the Suzuki method of violin playing. It's an uplifting story about something positive and beautiful that is happening in Nyanga, a township that is rife with crime and poverty:

MOZART IN NYANGA

The wind whips up dust circles on the streets of Nyanga, Cape Town's oldest township and home to over 10 000 people. People congregate on the streets: a man holds a woman's hand; a mother walks behind her three children wearing brightly coloured woollen caps; street vendors cook skewers of cow's intestines braaied over fires in tin drums. Goats saunter down the street.

The surprising sound of a bow being scraped slowly across a violin string accompanies this scene like a musical score to a movie. Follow the sound of Mozart's Twinkle Twinkle Little Star, played with a beginner's halting uncertainty, and you arrive at Hlengisa Primary School. Peer inside the window and you will see a group of six kids, violins tucked neatly under their chins.

It seems as if many centuries and cultures congregate in this small space. Not only are the children learning violin, but they are being taught the instrument through the revolutionary Suzuki method, developed by the Japanese master who has gained worldwide acclaim for his innovative teaching methods. South Africa has only a handful of violinists who have undergone the rigorous three-year training to qualify as Suzuki teachers. Among them is Maria Bothes, who returned to South Africa after spending 23 years at one of Europe's foremost training centres. Now, she's employed by the Cape Philharmonic Orchestra as project manager for the Masidlale (Let us Play) outreach program that provides violin lessons to 80 children in Nyanga and Gugelethu townships.

Initially, Maria had to be careful not to tread on the local school teachers' toes. Not all of them saw the value of pupils missing 'proper' lessons to fiddle about with an instrument. But despite some misgivings, they sacrificed their staffroom to create space for the children to practice. Although having people wander in and out to make coffee is occasionally disturbing, Maria welcomes the exposure as it has allowed the teachers to witness the children's efforts and created a family atmosphere.

The Suzuki method develops children's musicality through listening and feeling rather than engaging the intellect and teaching students to read music. As Maria says: "You go to notes, you go to the head." Suzuki teachers believe the instrument must become part of the student's body. Maria claims that people taught with rigid classical methods don't "feel the vibration of the violin going into their soul." The souls of Maria's students shine through the smiles that split their faces as they learn the rhythm of a piece of music by miming songololos. Their pleasure fills the staffroom. As we accompany the kids back to their classroom, Maria is everywhere greeted with cries of "Violin, violin!" One young boy hops in front of her, dramatically waving his arms back and forth, drawing an imaginary bow. "All the kids want to play music," says Maria.

The violin can offer a passport out of the township. Louis Heyneman, CEO of the Cape Town Philharmonic Orchestra, predicts that a future generation of CPO musicians will come from the townships. He believes that many of these kids have an innate musicality. In addition, some have the hunger derived from not being born with a silver spoon in their mouths. Take the boy who doesn't have a fourth finger, essential for playing the violin. He was so keen to play that Maria at first didn't have the heart to turn him away. When she eventually had to tell him that it would never be possible for her to teach him properly, undaunted he demonstrated that he could just manage to reach the string with the tiny stump of his finger.

While the possibility of a career as a professional musician is lucrative, Maria stresses that whatever the outcome, the process of learning to play the violin is worthwhile in itself. The lessons teach children, often traumatized by hardship and hunger, many valuable skills, including focus and co-ordination. Perhaps most important is the self-esteem that they gain from mastering a difficult task. According to Maria, learning the violin can even, almost magically, instil an ethical disposition. She believes that "no violinist can be a bad person; the violin creates goodness in you." Each centre has 20 violins that each cost R1500 and their safety is a concern. Already, in the year since Maria started giving lessons, the school has lost their computers in two burglaries. Each time Maria was relieved to find the violins untouched and safely locked away in a storage cupboard where they are packed between bags of rice and mealie meal.

Ten-year-old Sandiswe is one of Maria's most dedicated and promising students. When she first saw a violin, she was immediately fascinated and vowed that one day she would play in a concert on a stage. Currently, Sandiswe plays three times a week. To progress further she must work on her technique daily. There are plans to buy another 20 violins, some of which can be taken home to practice, but this raises a lot of dilemmas; would Sandiswe be safe walking home with the violin or would it perhaps make her vulnerable to attack from thieves?

Sandiswe lives with her grandmother, Momawelo, in a brick home, cold and damp but neat as a pin. Maria goes to meet Momawelo at her home to discuss the possibility of Sandiswe taking a violin home. "The violin will be safe," Momawelo assures Maria. She will store it on top of the wardrobe and Sandiswe's sister will accompany her from school. Momawelo welcomes the opportunity for Sandiswe to develop her talent but admits that the violin is not a sound she's used to. "Oh my God!" she exclaims, covering her ears at the prospect of Sandiswe rehearsing scales every night. But while learning the violin is a screechy process, I can imagine a time when Sandiswe has mastered the violin, and her music wafts through the township.

Maria believes that already the violins are bringing healing to the community: "What makes me think that love is hanging over the school, the kids, the staff, and sometimes the shacks outside? I guess it can't be explained rationally, but it seems to me that the overwhelming power of the energy that each child releases through the ringing notes of their melodies gently strokes the heart of the whole neighbourhood."

TASK: Spend the week immersed in reading human interest features.

Read these three classics:

1.   Anne Hull's Una Vida Mejore (A Better Life), especially part 2: The Smell of Money in *St. Petersburg Times*

2.   Gene Weineggar's Fatal Distraction in the *Washington Post*

3.   Katherine Boo's The Marriage Cure in the *New Yorker*

Clippings file

Collect 3 human interest features of varying lengths and complexity, from 800 words up to 5, 000 words. When you have selected your three favourites, print them and add them to your clippings file.

First person accounts

"The first step is to acquire some distance from yourself. If you are panicked by any examination of your flaws, you will not get very far in the writing of personal essays. You need to be able to see yourself from the ceiling, know how you are coming across in social situations, and accurately assess when you charm and when you seem pushy, mousy, or ridiculous. You must begin to take inventory of yourself so that you can present that self to the reader as a specific, legible character.

Start with your quirks – the idiosyncrasies, stubborn tics, and anti-social mannerisms that set you apart from others. To establish credibility, resist coming across as average. Who wants to read about the regular Joe? Many beginning essayists try so hard to be likeable and nice, to fit in, that the reader – craving stronger stuff, a tone of authority, - gets bored. Restraining one's expressiveness, smoothing ones edges, or sparing everyone's feelings will not work on the page. Literature is not a place for conformists."

Phillip Lopate in *Telling True Stories*

First person accounts are features in which the narrators experience is the story. They are generally written in the first person present with an aim to taking the reader as close to the experience as possible. The essence of good first-person narrative is sharing an experience, letting the reader see, touch, taste and feel it. Often the writer takes the reader on a journey which ends an 'aha' moment.

Often unusual or exhilarating activities, such as skydiving or shark cage diving, will be the subject of first person accounts. Another convention is "My day as a..." when the writer tries an obscure, difficult or taboo occupation. Sometimes these first person accounts serve a deeper purpose of revealing injustice. For example, Mac McClelland's I Was a Warehouse Wage Slave, which highlights the terrible working conditions endured by order fulfilment staff in mega-warehouses in America.

George Plimpton made his name writing first person accounts and established the genre of what is called participatory Journalism. In the 1960's he played professional football for the Detroit Lions, stepped into the ring to fight a professional boxer, was a trapeze artist for a circus, and played triangle for the New York Philharmonic. Attributed to the up-for-anything Plimpton is the maxim "I have never been convinced there's anything inherently wrong in having fun." Plimpton's contemporary, Corey Levitan wrote a Fear and Loafing column for the Las Vegas Review-Journal, in which he tries and writes about a different occupation, hobby, or lifestyle every week. He's tried his hand as an optometrist, bailiff, birthday clown, sushi chef, prison guard and umpire. He explains, "I do activities that the audience is familiar with, but I bring in new elements of education and comedy that they hadn't thought of," says Levitan. "Some of the activities are unique, like being a madam at a Las Vegas Chicken Ranch, but it's not that important that it be a unique job. The key is to find unique situations and angles in any job or lifestyle, even if it's a mundane or trivial task."

The amount of reporting required by a first person account varies. You should establish from your editor what they want. For example, the sample below – Hope on a Rope - includes very little facts about Table Mountain and could have been expanded to include geological and meteorological information.

The first person account is easily adapted into a general feature. For example, the story about the wage slave could easily become the starting point of a general feature exploring the exploitation of workers in factories.

Never forget that in first persona accounts you are a character in your own writing. Unlike in interview pieces, when you are backstage, you are in the spotlight. You need to remember when you are writing from the first person that you are creating a persona, a character. The real you, sorry to say, is probably a bit boring, more Walter Mitty than James Bond.

Hope on a rope – abseiling on Table Mountain.

Walking backward off a 1km-tall mountain is kind of counterintuitive, to say the least.

But it's what Gareth Gibson persuades people to do on a daily basis. Makes you wonder what he could achieve if he employed his demonic powers of persuasion for more practical purposes. I hadn't thought much about abseiling, adopting the same kind of feet-first, brain-later approach that had characterized my life so far. I'd been so busy persuading my abseiling companion that everything would be fine that I'd forgotten to think about how it would be for me.

I really don't like heights. Sometimes I get vertigo when I stand up too quickly. And so, when Gareth starts the safety demonstration and I step into the harness, I suddenly get an OMG kind of feeling.

Gareth talks a lot about facing fears. He's funny. I remember laughing, quite hysterically actually – hahaheeheee – even when he wasn't telling jokes. Apparently, love is best induced in experiences that produce fear. Rollercoaster rides and ski slopes are all known aphrodisiacs. Gareth is actually really very attractive. I think I'm falling in love with Gareth.

Oops, no, I'm falling off a mountain. Silly me. The thing about walking backwards over a mountain ledge is that you just don't know what to expect. At the root of all fear is a primal terror of the unknown. Therefore, I try to neutralize my anxiety by calmly taking my mind through what will happen when I step off the edge. This proves to be a mistake, because when I consider it rationally, I conclude that I will flip upside down, fall out of my harness and crash head first to the bottom of Table Mountain.

By now, I'm beginning to regret this idea.

We traipse along, tied together like convicts, pressing ourselves like paper against the rock behind a ledge which, according to Gareth, is the most hugged piece of rock in the world.

Facing one's fears is a noble activity, but surely best undertaken in private. Above us a large group of spectators has gathered.

I have taken a wrong turn. I'm always the one who watches. How did I get here? But there is no turning back. Any notion of changing my mind is ruled out by an unwillingness to appear cowardly before my public. How weird is the brain? It's a miracle that our species ever managed to survive, given that we'd opt for flinging ourselves off a mountain rather than admit public defeat.

If you've seen that scene in Dead Man Walking, you'll know how I feel now. It goes against your every instinct to walk backward into oblivion. Suddenly I'm squeezing my rope like a last hope. Gareth tells us to keep breathing and my friend and I are exhaling like rhinos on heat. Then suddenly our feet are no longer beneath us, but in front of us. We have stepped off the mountain!

There's no danger with abseiling.

I was told that the 112m controlled descent would last between four to seven minutes.

It seemed so much longer. Halfway down, the rock falls away from my feet and I drop into nothingness, bouncing like a baby in a harness. For the first time, gravity is my friend; I float in my amniotic space sac, enjoying an unsurpassed view of rock, ocean, city and sky, before being lowered, Rapunzel like, safely to the ground. What was all the fuss about?

TASK: Spend the week immersed in reading first person accounts.

Read these three classics:

1. The Story of an Eyewitness: The San Francisco Earthquake, by Jack London in Collier's Weekly, 1906.

2. Mac McClelland's I Was a Warehouse Wage Slave, in Mother Jones magazine

3. Into Thin Air, by Jon Krakauer

Clippings File

Collect 3 first person account features of varying lengths an complexity, from 800 words up to 5, 000 words. When you have selected your three favourites, print them and add them to your clippings file.

General features and Narrative features

"For some subjects, not choosing narrative means not being read at all. When your subjects are grim and your characters destitute, disabled, or extremely unintelligent and the wrongs against them are complicated, how many people are going to relish tucking into your story with their bagels and cream cheese on a Sunday morning? I choose narrative, sometimes with ambivalence, to further the goal of our profession: readers finishing the story and maybe giving half a damn."

Katherine Boo, in *Telling True Stories*

Many features can't be easily categorized and might best be called general features. These stories investigate social phenomenon and often hang on the news peg of proximity and relevance. They tend to make the reader say to themselves, "who knew". For example, Fantastic Plastic, a story in South Africa's Mail and Guardian, explored the empowering impact that Tupperware has had on South African women for the last 50 years. South Africa's Tupperware queen, Betty Moreroa, broke the world sales record in 2011 by selling R2.5 million Rands worth of Tupperware in one month. Wow!

It's easy to recognize the general feature, but difficult to define. It's the soft news that tells a story, using literary techniques such as vivid description. Common to these features are delayed ledes that, unlike summary news ledes, draw the reader into the story without explaining the vital who and what elements of the story.

Narrative, or long form features, occupy the echelons of feature writing. They are making a recent comeback. Initially people thought that the internet would mean the death of long form journalism, predicting that no-one would want to read lengthy pieces on a computer screen. There was a belief that the digital world was only for accessing quick bursts of information. In fact, there has been a heightened interest in long-form which people enjoy reading on their smart phones and tablets.

Dawn Kennedy penetrates the tattoo lover's world, a place where pain, pleasure and permanence meet.

Close your eyes and you could be at the dentist. The ink pen, the tool of the tattoo artist's trade, makes a surprisingly loud and intimidating drone as it's switched on for the first time. It's used to make a 1.5mm deep puncture in the skin, into which tiny amounts of indelible ink are deposited. Master tattoo artist Manuela is numb to its pneumatic noise. Having heard it for innumerable hours, she finds it a comforting, familiar sound. So much so that she says, "I get uneasy if I don't hear it."

Sonja Myberg is having a geisha, the epitome of refined Japanese femininity, tattooed on her inner arm, stretching between the wrist and elbow. This, her eighth tattoo, is a Sailor Jerry design. Sonja is employed by the rum label named after the iconic ink artist and today's inscription is a display of loyalty to the brand. This is her first time with Manuela. While some people remain with one tattoo artist, Sonja wears work on her body from seven different artists in Cape Town. She says, "I'm collecting art."

How long did it take her to decide on the design, I wonder? "One second," she replies. Seeing my shock that someone could so arbitrarily incise a major percentage of her epidermis, Manuela explains there are two camps of people: "Those who are impulsive and those who obsess endlessly over their design." Today's tattoo is no mere star on the arm, but a major undertaking that will take more than three hours of non-stop skin puncturing.

The confined upstairs space where Manuela works offers a bird's-eye view of Long Street, but once Manuela starts to tattoo she focuses fiercely on the 30cm of Sonja's inner arm and the bustling business of the street outside fades to insignificance. Although there's a lot of easy conversation, there is an undercurrent of solemnity to the occasion, befitting the fact that, after today, Sonja's appearance will be irrevocably (bar complicated and expensive skin grafting) changed.

Tattooing, it seems to me, dramatizes the inevitable process of being scarred by a world that inexorably makes its mark on us. Which one of us wants to pass through life untouched, unscathed? We long for contact and tattooing seems like a willing participation in the pain that contact inevitably entails. Used ritualistically, tattooing marks time, skills acquired, social status. Gang, prison and tribal tattoos are a script that can be read. But in the secular world tattooing marks a moment of consciousness, an impulse of affiliation with an image. Aptly the folder of artwork of tattoo designs is called "flash" art. But in its impulsiveness lies its beauty. There's daring in it. The same daring of the young couple at the altar who swear "I do". This defiant (or unconscious) willingness to bet on permanence, in a world that to all rational evidence is transient, makes tattooing a gesture towards a willingness to commit that in other areas of life is praised as a sign of maturity and depth of character.

Manuela interrupts my introspection to reassure Sonja that if the pain becomes too much, they can take two sessions to complete the tattoo. But Sonja replies, "I can't do that; it's gotta be done."

With the tattoo outlined onto Sonya's arm, Manuela lowers the ink pen to make its first puncture on the skin. "Well, here we go. You're no stranger to this," she says. Pain is definitely part of the process. Some people cry; some faint – but that's more often from low blood sugar or anxiety than the actual pain. Manuela explains that fear is the biggest obstacle for the newcomer. "People don't want to look like a sissy – that's the problem. Breathing, really, is the key." And the pain is subjective. Some describe it as an irritating prickle; others say that the discomfort afterwards, when the tattoo is scabbing and healing, is worse.

For certain sectors of society, tattoos are a symbol that you are tough enough not to mind the pain. For those with masochistic inclinations, pain is the pleasurable point. One anonymous person confessed about their tattoo: "My first and only one is on the right side of my pelvis. The artist kept hitting bone, which vibrated through my whole body... It hurt soooo good! After it was done, I had the best sex of my life – weak legs, shaky hands and blurred vision. I'm planning on getting another one and I'm looking forward to the pain."

For the first hour, Sonja is upbeat, wincing occasionally when the needle goes closer to the more sensitive areas. "It's amazing how different it feels on each part of the body," she remarks.

Manuela's most noticeable tattoo is the spider that adorns her neck. But she definitely doesn't fit the profile of a hard-core tattoo artist. Bent over Sonja, working serenely, she explains, "I didn't come into tattooing from a rebellious point. I'm not a biker. I'm drawn to the artistry, and it was my mission to show people that there are many other sides to tattooing." That mission took her all over the world in a quest to prepare for the first Cape Town Tattoo convention in 2009. "Tattoo conventions allow the public into a secret world," Manuela explains. "They can come and watch amazing work being done. In a convention tattooing becomes like performance art."

.....

During the five minutes she is gone, Manuela barely shifts position. She admits that the spider's web on her neck sets her apart from the other mothers at the exclusive private school that her daughter attends. She's not often asked to bake cakes, but rather given the task of body painting the kids in the school play.

As Sonja returns reluctantly to the ophthalmic chair that looks like a suitable torture device, she confides, "The first hour is like thumbs-up; the rest is downhill." Manuela has outlined the tattoo in black and is colouring in now. "It's like oil painting. You use the darker colours first," she explains. Towards the end of the second hour the upbeat mood begins to darken. Sonja becomes noticeably tense, wriggling in the chair and tapping her foot with irritation. She calls for another cigarette break. Manuela wraps her arm in cling film. "You can always come back," she suggests to Sonja, who replies, "Don't want to."

The third hour is definitely tense. Manuela has hardly moved. I'm in awe of her focus and commend her patience. She tells me, "I'm an Aries and not patient in general. People who know me can't believe what I do." As the third hour passes, Sonja is struggling. Skunk n Nancy's *Weak* blares through the speakers: "Weak as I am, no tears for you; deep as I am, I'm no one's fool." As Manuela works towards the sensitive area in her elbow, Sonja says, "I won't be able to sit through that." Manuela reassures her quietly, "You can." As pain takes centre stage, everyone is quiet. "I can't do it. I just feel sorry for myself," says Sonja close to tears. "Suck it up," says Manuela, handing her a Fizzer. It's an old trick that soothes Sonja until her arm begins to tremble. "I'm starting to shake. Do you have a ball I can hold?" Manuela gives her a wad of crumpled tissue.

Through her discomfort, Sonja tells Manuela, "You do it much softer compared to the other tattooists – especially the way you wipe – that constant wiping drives me berserk." After three and a half hours, Sonja can take no more. The geisha's tiny lotus blossom feet will have to wait for another day. As though the school bell has rung on Friday afternoon, she leaps from the seat.

"Oh that's amazing" she says, admiring her arm. "Now all I have to do is give her a name."

Read the full article: www.dawnkennedywriter.com

TASK. Spend the week immersed in reading general and narrative features.

1.   Wall Street on the Tundra, Michael Lewis in Vanity Fair

2.   Have You Ever Tried to Sell a Diamond? Edward Jay Epstein, the Atlantic

3.   In the Jungle, Rian Malan, in Rolling Stone

Clippings file

Collect 3 profile features of varying lengths an complexity, from 800 words up to 5, 000 words. When you have selected your three favorites, print them and add them to your clippings file.

Reviews

"For all criticism is based on that equation: knowledge + taste = meaningful judgment. The key word here is meaningful. People who have strong reactions to a work—and most of us do—but don't possess the wider erudition that can give an opinion heft, are not critics. (This is why a great deal of online reviewing by readers isn't criticism proper.) Nor are those who have tremendous erudition but lack the taste or temperament that could give their judgment authority in the eyes of other people, people who are not experts. (This is why so many academic scholars are no good at reviewing for mainstream audiences.) Like any other kind of writing, criticism is a genre that one has to have a knack for, and the people who have a knack for it are those whose knowledge intersects interestingly and persuasively with their taste. In the end, the critic is someone who, when his knowledge, operated on by his taste in the presence of some new example of the genre he's interested in—a new TV series, a movie, an opera or ballet or book—hungers to make sense of that new thing, to analyse it, interpret it, make it mean something."

Daniel Mendelsohn in the *New Yorker*

Almost every publication, whether online or in print, dedicates a section to some form of reviewing, criticism or appraisal. Why should so much print and space be devoted to this activity? Culture, and commentary upon it, is a vital part of our days. Whilst many decry the decline of culture, open any magazine you will find film and book reviews. Admittedly the classic arts such as ballet, opera and classical music are being jostled aside to accommodate our growing passion for film reviews. And food. No longer simply a means of sustenance, eating has become a cultural activity. Nowadays, people "go out to eat" as they once went out to the opera. And just as previously they wanted to know whether their trip to the opera would be worthwhile, now they want guidance, criticism and reviews to help them decide which restaurant to book for the evening. The rise of the celebrity chef has led to the rise of the celebrity restaurant which has resulted in the rise of the celebrity reviewer.

How do you place food and theatre in the same category? Admittedly it's difficult. However, whatever you review requires firstly that you are willing to hold an opinion.

Reviewing is the act of taking a stand and arguing the evidence for it. Looked at in this way, it doesn't matter whether you are reviewing a meal at the legendary Le Meurice in Paris, or Snoop Dogs latest album, the question addressed in a review is what is your opinion about it?

However, this is where a lot of beginner reviewers stall. Students are quick to give an opinion: This book/film/album was "awesome" or "boring," they declare confidently. But when asked why they deem it so, to give evidence, they get stuck.

Just as a first person account is not about you, but about an activity filtered through your experience, so a review is not about your knee jerk reaction. You need to view the book, film or food in context. All art is either elaborating on, or reacting to, tradition. When you are reviewing you need to assess the subject of your review in context of that tradition. This is fairly evident in the visual arts and literature, but equally applies to food. Compare and contrast Heston Blumenthal's and Noma's chef René Redzepi's approach to food. One is modernist, embracing chemicals and the other is traditionalist spearheading the movement back to wild food. Each of these two approaches is valid. As William Zinsser says in, *On Writing Well* "Criticism is a serious intellectual act. It tries to evaluate serious works of art and to place them in the context of what has been done before in that medium or by that artist."

Also, all art is created with an intended purpose and needs to be evaluated according to whether the artist succeeds or fails in their intentions. Artists are either striving for novelty or yearning for tradition. Each holds an individual aesthetic and value scale and has to be assessed according to their intention.

If this makes you feel daunted, good. Far too many people are willing to offer shabbily written reviews filled with flabby, often damming criticism without making any effort to understand the director, writer or painter's intention.

Recently a student experienced how taking time to research a director's intentions changed her attitude to the film, *Noah*, which she was reviewing. Many online amateur commentators criticized the movie for diverging from Biblical accuracy. However, research revealed that this was the director's stated intention. This shifted her perspective on the movie and enabled her to appreciate it more.

I've spilt much ink as an art reviewer, starting with my stint reviewing art movies. I had no clue about art movies, but was sufficiently motivated to research different cinema traditions and understand the central role of noodles in Japanese movies. At various stages I've had to steep myself in different art forms, depending on what beat I was covering. At one stage, I was writing theatre reviews, at another book reviews. Perhaps most challenging was when I was assigned to write a series of profiles on emerging artists. In art, my taste tends towards the traditional. I'm not a fan of contemporary art. To write my pieces I followed Susan Sontag's advice, went "Against Interpretation" and paid attention to my own aesthetic responses to the artworks. I then asked the artists to discuss their work, to tell me what they were aiming for.

I always approached reviewing with humility and took the task seriously. It's much easier to lampoon myself in a first person account than write an honest review that is fair to a potential audience and the creator of the work.

If you have been close to any accomplished artists you will understand the immense effort that goes into any work of art, whatever the medium. Given the artists dedication, I feel it is incumbent on the reviewer to agonize over their review, to be aware of the moral weight of the act. I've always preferred to call myself an art appreciator rather than an art critic, with its suggestion of someone who is trying to find fault. I approach reviewing with a willingness to enjoy the experience. I would hate to be seen as the acerbic food critic in Ratatouille!

An exception to this is when my opinion goes against the grain, when I feel that the audience is being swept along on a wave of enthusiasm. One example was the highly popular The Syringa Tree. The author and performer gave a consummate performance. However, the story revolves around the grown woman's attempt to find the Nanny who disappeared after raising her during Apartheid in South Africa. For the girl the nanny reminded her of an idyllic time. The woman never questioned that the Nanny might not want to be found. She was blind to the imbalance of power in the relationship in a way that irked me.

Another example is a widely lauded rest The Test Kitchen which is madly popular in Cape Town. I dined there with renowned food critic Pru Leith. She enjoyed the experience but I didn't like the concept of industrial five star dining, dislike the whole notion of gentrification and felt awkward eating an expensive meal in an impoverished area. The waiters were male models who would clearly have preferred to be sipping cocktails by a poolside than carrying dishes to patrons.

Perhaps "Cause no harm" should be the first rule of reviewing – and living. Given the popularity of both these productions my criticism was like spitting in the wind and would have no ill effect other than possibly making people question their popularity.

Another rule for reviewers is that you should love what you review. If you can't bear to sit through an opera, don't for God's sake offer to review it. As Zinsser says, writing about film critics, "If you think movies are dumb, don't write about them. The reader deserves a movie buff that will bring along a reservoir of knowledge, passion and prejudice. It's not necessary for the critic to like every film; criticism is only one person's opinion. But he should go to every movie wanting to like it."

Love your medium is Zinsser's first rule of reviewing. His second is that reviewers should be careful not to give away too much of the plot. The internet has spawned a plethora of amateur reviewers all of which are happy to tell you that they didn't like it when the main character was killed at the end. Odious. This seems obvious for books and films, but it can be applied to art and food. If the artist wants to surprise the diner or viewer, don't spoil that surprise. For example, the highlight of a tasting menu at a wonderful restaurant was when one dish was brought spouting dry ice like Aladdin's Lamp. It elicited gasps from the patrons. I chose not to describe that moment in my review and to keep the surprise a secret for future diners.

Zinsser's final admonishment to reviewers is to use specific detail and follow the literary maxim of "Show don't tell." Don't tell me that the main character in a film is fascinating - describe in detail how heads turn in her direction when she walks into a room.

A good rule for writing in general, and especially in reviewing, is to avoid vague adjectives. Words like beautiful, compelling, and riveting mean different things to each reader. What specifically in the movie did you find beautiful or compelling? Every time you use an adjective, ask yourself, where's the evidence? Delete the adjective and leave the evidence instead. Your writing will be much stronger.

SAMPLE: Here's a critical review that I wrote about a popular play, The Syringa Tree:

The prospect of watching a play about a privileged South African girl reminiscing about her idyllic African childhood is not instantly appealing, but The Syringa Tree arrives trailing near-hysterical accolades from America and more muted praise from England. The opening scene of six-year old Elizabeth swinging on a tree against a backdrop of the infinite skies of Africa sent sighs surging through the audience. When she began to speak in imitation of a six-year-old I had to quell the urge to send her to her room.

However, director Larry Moss's insistence that actress Pamela Glen plays all 26 parts in this memoir play was a stroke of genius that rescued The Syringa Tree from the hackneyed *I had a Farm in Africa* genre. Glen gives an energized performance that squeezes every drop out of her craft. She manages to juggle 26 characters without alienating, boring or losing most of the audience whilst staying up way past her bedtime.

Glenn manages the transitions with consummate ease but realizes the characters of the mother, Salema and her daughter, Molisend, most convincingly. The portrayal of the father was weak. Her character list was possibly too crowded and the action could have been moved along better with fewer, more developed characters.

By getting under each character's skin, Glenn demonstrates a remarkable sleight of political hand. Glen's protean performance gives mixed messages. It says on the one hand: "This is my story. I am observing all of this and I am a young white South Africa girl."

On the other hand, it claims, "There is nothing that separates us. I can inhabit any skin. This is a universal story." It physically enacts what every aspiring writer hopes to achieve: Imbuing a personal story with universal appeal.

The ruse of narrating the story through the precocious Elizabeth presents Apartheid in stark and shocking terms. Elizabeth watches from her bedroom window at night as police brutally beat a man who doesn't have a pass. The violence is amplified when seen through innocent eyes.

It's fascinating watching a young girl trying to make sense of this world. From an early age she understands that "Some things are allowed and some things are not." Her nanny, Salima, gives birth to a daughter, Molisend, who the family houses illegally, keeping her hidden. Elizabeth treats this like a game, chanting, "Molisend, hideaway" like a nursery rhyme. But her anxiety is revealed through unconscious gestures. Horrified by hearing that the gardener had his fingers chopped off, Elizabeth tugs at the ends of her fingers and makes chopping motions.

The young girl us surrounded by Xhosa, Sotho, Afrikaans, English and Jewish culture. These diverse cultures are brought to life through songs rendered with gusto. Scenes of domestic bliss are signified with classical music. The songs are not just entertaining, but convey the soul of the different cultures.

I loved the sense of rhythm that pulses through the play. At one point, Elizabeth slaps her thighs and chest in syncopated rhythm and careens around the stage chanting," The drums, the drums." The drumbeat echoing through the night sky is an evocative symbol of Africa. Later the symbol is skillfully transmuted when the father tells Elizabeth that America is the land of the brave and free and that if she listens to her heartbeat she can hear it beating those words.

The sub-text of the play is Elizabeth's quest to find out where her heart really lies – does it beat to an African or an American rhythm?

The core of The Syringa Tree explores the relationship between Salima and Elizabeth. Salima is trapped in a subtle web of emotional entanglement that the audience is supposed to swallow as love. After as tragic killing, Salima disappears. The reason for this is never explained. The mother wrings her hands and gives what sounds like a display of bourgeois pique: "They work for you for years and years. Treat them like one of your own and then they disappear, just like that."

I found the final reunion scene excruciating. I was not persuaded that Salima would be pleased to see Elizabeth rocking up on her doorstep after all those years. At any point she could have chosen to make contact with her former employers. Elizabeth never questions what Salima wants or wonders why she chose to work for another family.

The Syringa Tree is dripping with emotion and contains some exceptionally powerful scenes. However, it is handicapped by an overemphasis on the benevolence of Elizabeth's family and a determinedly sentimental interpretation of her relationship with Salima.

The play is brilliantly performed and directed but the idea that it tells, as it proclaims, a tale that transcends racial boundaries, is absurd. Elizabeth and Salima make gestures of friendship across a very safe racial divide. Ultimately, this is polished white liberalism wrestling with guilt.

TASK. Spend the week immersed in reading reviews.

Read these three classics:

1.   L'ami Louis by AA Gill in Vanity Fair

2.   Almost Famous by Roger Ebert

3.   Novel of the Year by Daniel Mendelsohn, reviewing The Lovely
Bones in the New York Review of Books.

Clippings file

Collect 3 reviews of varying lengths and complexity, from 800 words up to
5, 000 words. When you have selected your three favorites, print them
and add them to your clippings file.

Travel features

"If 19th-century travel writing was principally about place - about filling in the blanks of the map and describing remote places that few had seen - the best 21st-century travel writing is almost always about people: exploring the extraordinary diversity that still exists in the world beneath the veneer of globalization. As Jonathan Raban once remarked: "Old travellers grumpily complain that travel is now dead and that the world is a suburb. They are quite wrong. Lulled by familiar resemblances between all the unimportant things, they meet the brute differences in everything of importance."

William Dalrymple, *The Guardian*,

Travel writing, at its most basic, describes places and people in detail. Travel writing is usually written in the first person and can be considered a special example of a first person account. The writer uses descriptive and imaginative language and makes his thoughts and feelings about a place clear.

SAMPLE: Here's a travel feature that I wrote about leopard tracking at Bushman's Kloof:

A PASSION FOR PREDATORS: Dawn Kennedy takes a civilized walk with wild cats at Bushman's Kloof

A person diminishes amid the Cederberg's landscape of sedimentary rock, sandstone and shale. Jagged stones stand like ancient tombs, paying tribute to the glacier that scraped the exposed rock, 340 million years ago.

Evidence of geological time immemorial makes one's own personal biography a meaningless blip. Goal-setting, striving and daily dramas seem absurd viewed against this backdrop. As we lose cell phone reception, the false web of online intimacy dissipates. My mind goes blank and settles on a hallucinatory appreciation of the landscape – rocks turn to people, dragons and reptiles.

Yet, despite appearing impenetrable, humans have managed to have a negative impact on this landscape. Large numbers of the cedar trees that baptized this region were felled for construction: 7200 trees were used as telephone poles between Piketberg and Calvinia. Fires added to the destruction until the removal of dead cedar trees was banned in 1967. All other exploitation ended in 1973 with the proclamation of the Cederberg Wilderness. In 2004, the Cederberg Wilderness received World Heritage Site status as part of the Cape Floral Region.

Combine this area's natural credentials with Bushman's Kloof, voted the best hotel in the world in 2009 by Travel and Leisure, USA, and you have a heady combination. In fact, it's surreal. While the landscape makes you feel puny, as though it could swallow you in one gulp, the delightful staff at Bushman's Kloof makes every effort to restore your sense of importance. You matter enough to be offered a sherry on arrival, to have your linen turned down, a piece of chocolate and bedtime story on your pillow and your name known to every staff member.

Here the borderline between the human and the animal feels flimsy, as though you could step from one realm into the other. This is leopard country. Among the estimated less-than-1000 roaming Cape leopards, 35 of them live here, perfectly at home in the rocky mountain ranges.

Our weekend begins with a sunset drive. We see blesbok, gemsbok, and even an African hare with its oversize ears illuminated by the setting sun. However, the animals that we are here to track – the leopard and caracal – remain elusive. I know the odds of seeing either are minimal and too much to hope for, but I do so all the same, gluing my eyes to the rugged horizon.

Somewhere in the cracks and fissures of this rugged landscape, 35 leopards are getting ready to stalk the animals that we watch with delight and, click-whirr, capture on celluloid. Some unfortunate ones might be captured later by a leopard in another way.

Seppi, our Namibian ranger, pulls up by the purple stained lake, arranges a bar, and offers us gin and tonics, complete with ice and a slice of lemon. As the gin warms my throat, I revel in my position at the top of the food chain. Sipping slowly, details in the red landscape come alive: mossy outcrops like miniature Zen gardens cover rock surfaces and bright pink flowers, like sudden gasps of beauty, push through invisible cracks in the rock.

Read the full story: www.dawnkennedywriter.com

TASK: Spend the week immersed in reading travel features.

Read these three classics:

1. My London, and Welcome by A A Gill in the New York Times

2. A Supposedly Fun Thing I'll Never Do Again, David Foster Wallace's account of a luxury Caribbean cruise, in Essays and Arguments

3. Forbidden by Tim Cahill in Outside magazine

Clippings file

Collect 3 different types of travel feature. When you have selected your three favorites, print them and add them to your clippings file.

Columnists

"Columnists usually start out full of juice, sounding like terrific boulevardiers and raconteurs, retailing in print all the marvellous mots and anecdotes they have been dribbling away over lunch for the past few years. After eight or ten weeks, however, they start to dry up. You can see the poor bastards floundering and gasping. They're dying of thirst. They're out of material. They start writing about funny things that happened around the house the other day, homey one-liners that the better half or the Avon Lady got off, or some fascinating book or article that got them thinking, or else something they saw on the TV. Thank God for the TV! Without television shows to cannibalise, half of these people would be lost, utterly catatonic. Pretty soon you can see it, the tubercular blue of the 23-inch screen, radiating from their prose."

Tom Wolfe

Despite Wolfe's cynical assessment, columns provide some of the most pleasurable reading in media. Columnists are often the stars of the media, bringing wit and personality to the publication they write for and gaining a loyal following.

There are several categories of columnists:

Advice columns

Offering advice on beauty, health, finance, relationships etc.

Gossip columns

Keeping readers informed about who's who in the society zoo.

Pundit columns

Deep thinking opinion mongers offering trenchant opinions on the issues of the day.

Specialist columns

Experts called in to provide commentary and expert analysis on current news events.

Personal columns

This type of column is written in a warm conversational style, sharing the intimacies of everyday life. What could be simpler, writing about yourself? But these personal columns are deceptively difficult. The problem, as Wolf parodies in the quote opening this segment, is running out of steam.

TASK: Spend the week immersed in reading columns.

Read these two classics:

1. Norah Ephron, I feel Bad about my Neck, a collection of columns.

2. My Bra's Too Tight and It's Never Too Late, by Paige Williams in O magazine

Clippings file

Collect 3 columns of varying lengths an complexity, from 800 words up to 5, 000 words. When you have selected your three favorites, print them and add them to your clippings file.

Trend features

A trend feature describes a series of events and traces them to a common cause or causes.

The key to writing a trend story is understanding the cause-and-effect relationships in the subject area, and being able to describe them clearly for readers. Most trend stories focus on one link in an extensive chain of cause and effect.

No one forgets their first time. "It's like your first kiss, though hardly something every girl dreams about," said Lilli Beard, 19, an incoming freshman at an Ivy League university, recalling her first "grind" at the tender age of 13.

Grinding, an overtly sexual dance, leaves many girls uncomfortable.

TASK: Spend the week immersed in reading trend features.

Read these two classics:

1.   A. G. Sulzberger In Small Towns, Gossip Moves to the Web, and Turns Vicious The New York Times

2.   Monocles: the latest made-up fashion trend by Hadley Freeman, in The Guardian

Collect 3 trend features of varying lengths an complexity, from 800 words up to 5, 000 words. When you have selected your three favorites, print them and add them to your clippings file.

Information features/service features

These lifestyle features are staples of magazines, websites and increasingly newspapers. Known as "news readers can use," they offer practical advice on a range of topics that will appeal to the target audience of the publication.

As well as being educational and informing, the best are entertaining, without marring the seriousness of the issue they are exploring.

Information features often begin with the phrase, where to... (Where to vacation with young children, Where to buy gold coins etc.).

Information features are clearly structured. They tend to be written in sub-headings, with information given in similar size blocks. The sub-headings follow logically, with the advice increasing in complexity.

Another common information feature is the list feature: The list feature was inflated to extremes by Patricia Schultz's 1,000 Places to See Before You Die.

One category of the information feature deserves special mention – the how-to feature. These include the straightforward how to something type of feature. For example:- How to Ace a First Date or How-to Bake a Perfect Apple Pie. However, this format is used to explore more serious issues, such as office bullying and rhino poaching.

How-to features have their own rules for writing, which are explored in the how-to write a how-to article.

SAMPLE: Here's a how-to feature that I wrote for Longevity:

When it comes to health, men are definitely the weaker sex. So, how can we help keep our partners in tip-top shape?

The longevity gap between the sexes is astonishing. In the lucky few who live to be over 100, women outnumber men nine to one. The average man lives a shorter life than the average woman, and for 15 years of that life he can expect to be seriously or chronically ill. These dismal statistics could very well be attributed to the fact that most males act as though they are invincible and engage in far more risky behaviour than women. They smoke more, drink more and drive faster than women and, to top it all, they are likely to visit a doctor only if a limb is hanging from a socket.

Contd.

The rest of the article is divided into sub-headings: how to get him to see a podiatrist; how to get him to see an optometrist etc.

CHAPTER 3: SELLING FEATURES

"Becoming a successful magazine writer starts with the idea. No matter how good a writer you might be, if you're not adept at coming up with article ideas, you have little or no chance of making it as a magazine writer. In part, this is a practical matter. You can't simply approach a magazine editor and say, 'Look, I'm a great writer. Come up with an idea for me and I'll prove it to you.' It just doesn't work that way.

The process is simple. You come up with an idea. You make sure it's focused. You match it with the appropriate magazine. You write a query letter. You send it to the appropriate editor. You wait for the answer."

Charles Salzberg in *The Portable MFA in Creative Writing*

Coming Up With Ideas

Magazines and websites are always on the lookout for the next big idea.

If you can come up with fresh ideas for a publication, you will be an editor's best friend. Off-course, in reality there are no new ideas and most of the features inside the covers of a publication are a variation of a theme. However, writing for magazines does require that you are something of a visionary. Not only do you need to be in touch with what is happening right here, right now, but as most print publications are planned three months ahead, you will need to anticipate what will be happening in the future. This is weirdly disorientating and puts you out of synch with the rest of the world. You will find yourself researching turkey recipes and ways to recycle Christmas paper long before December. And when the Christmas tree has been taken down, it's time to think about novel ways to paint Easter eggs. Websites tend to be more immediate, so if you prefer living in the present, writing online might be a better option.

I need to warn you. Chances are that before you started to think about writing features, life was fairly peaceful. You went to a concert, had a good time listening to the music, went home, fell asleep. Once you become a busy feature writer, those days are over. Your waking hours will be filled with thinking what next to write about. The extent of your obsession will depending on which end of the obsessive scale you occupy. Perhaps you can turn your mind off over the weekend or perhaps the thinking will rarely stop.

So, how do get the fountain stream of ideas to start gushing? Here are a few suggestions:

Start with your own experience

John McPhee says, "There are zillions of ideas out there—they stream by like neutrons. What makes somebody pluck forth one thing—a thing you're going to be spending as much as three years with? If I went down a list of all the pieces I ever had in The New Yorker, upward of ninety percent would relate to things I did when I was a kid. I've written about three sports—I played all of them in high school. I've written a great deal about the environment, about the outdoors-—that's from thirteen years at Keewaydin, in Vermont, where I went to camp every summer, first as a camper and then as a counselor. I'd go on canoe trips, backpacking trips, out in the woods all summer, sleeping on the ground."

McPhee's statement affirms the adage, write what you know. There is wisdom in this advice. You know so much more that you think you know. Examine your life. What have you done? Young people have less life experience to draw on but so many firsts take place before the age of twenty: first kiss; first date; first love; final school exams; finding a place at college; first job interview; first part time job; buying your first car and leaving home are all significant, life changing experiences that can be turned into features.

Talk to others

Again McPhee has invaluable advice: "When I was starting out, I said to friends, I'm looking for ideas. And a high-school friend named Bob VanDeventer said, why don't you write about the Pine Barrens? And I said, the what? I was born and raised in New Jersey, but I'd never heard of them. So VanDeventer starts telling me about the pines, and how there were holes in the ground that had no bottom. And that the people who lived there were odd, to put it mildly. He had a whole lot of things that he had learned somewhere about the Pine Barrens, and with respect for my good friends Bob, all of these things were wrong. But what he did was light the spark. It was in New Jersey, and it related to the woods, two things that I was interested in."

The easiest and most overlooked way of coming up with story ideas is to ask other people if they have any good ideas for stories. People are often burning with issues that they would love journalists to explore. Often these are injustices. For example, in South Africa our telecommunications company, Telkom, is an endless source of gripes. One day a friend pointed out that while customers pay for the fastest internet many areas can't provide it, something mentioned in the small print. As he tells me this, I'm seeing a possible feature.

On another occasion, I asked a work colleague for suggestions of what to write about. She told me about a serious issue that she they were battling with in her community – the children of Tik addicts. She explained that while the emphasis was on rehabilitating the drug addicts, often the addicts had kids that received no help and who were unmanageable at school and uncared for at home. This would make an excellent feature.

Find your niche

It's overwhelming, not to say impossible, to keep up with everything. An effective approach to freelancing is to find a niche topic that you are interested in. You don't need to be an expert in this field – remember that as a feature writer your task is to approach other experts, but it should be an area that you are interested in. For example, playing the stock market, investing in gold and social media are all hot niche topics.

Subscribe

Mailing lists are a great way to come up with new ideas. Obviously you can't subscribe to every mailing list or you would be swamped. Spend a month dedicating your time to between one and three topics. Subscribe to as many newsletters as possible that deal with your topics. Then at the end of the month review these topics. Do they still appeal? Delete the ones that don't from your list and find others to replace them.

Google alerts

Set a Google alert for every topic that you are interested in. Create a file on your desktop and store any mails and newsletters that you receive that interest you.

Read magazines

You need to read mainstream magazines. This is as much so that you know what ideas are dead. Once a feature has been written in a mainstream publication then it is no longer fresh and an editor will not be interested if you pitch it.

Read community newspapers

These often have articles about interesting local people that can spark ideas for human interest stories for more mainstream press.

Read trade journals

Often these are quarterly publications and can be delivered free. They are usually boring and badly written, but as they have a specialized, limited readership and you can glean ideas from them to pitch to a broader readership.

Read the small stuff

Stories that are given a small space in the paper can be developed into longer features. Keep an eye on court cases.

Cruise social media

Spend time daily keeping in touch with what is trending on social media sites. Beware that this is a potential brain and time brain. Set yourself a limited period of, say, 30 minutes per day and try to stick to it.

Watch the calendar

Anniversary dates are a good news peg for feature stories. Obviously this includes Valentine's Day, Ramadan and Yom Kippur but there are a plethora of international days, ranging from the serious Water day and Cancer day to silly ones, such as the Naked Cycling Day. Remember that you need to pitch your ideas well in advance of these dates.

Check out the hobbies section of the yellow pages

You will find many interesting ideas and sources for a variety of features.

TASK: Ideas are evanescent. They come, unbidden, at the strangest times and they seem so compelling that you are certain that you will never forget them. You will forget them.

Purchase an ideas file that you keep at home, or in your office.

In addition, you need something portable. The moleskin journals are great. Keep one in your handbag and one by the side of the bed.

TASK:

What you will need:

The centre fold of an old broad side of a newspaper

Thick marker pens

On the outside fold of the paper, spend ten minutes making a list of all the things that you have done in your life. Don't think, just write. Your list will look something like this:

Lived in a small town

Volunteered in on old people's home.

Went to study anatomy at college.

Renounced my religion

Etc.

Now, circle five of the events that had the most impact on your life.

Now, in the centre of a double page spread newspaper evenly space these 5 events inside bubbles.

Now, consider each event in turn and surround it with these phrases: Things I learned from…, Tips for…, and How To…

Can you find any possible feature stories?

Ten Things I Learned from Leaving a Small Town?

How to Keep an Elderly Person Company?

Topics need an angle

We have seen that writing for magazines is formulaic and that articles are written in specific formats. But that's not all. When asked to come up with ideas, students often propose topics, for example, tattooing, rap music etc. That's fine far as it goes, but rap music is a topic and insufficiently focused for a feature. Features need what is called an angle, a tight focus, or what writer Anne Lamott calls "the one-inch frame." A topic becomes a story idea when it has what is known as an angle. Angle can be defined as a specific approach. It answers the question "So what?" An effective piece of writing establishes a single focus and sustains that focus throughout the piece. Just as a photographer needs to focus on a particular subject to produce a clear picture, a writer needs to focus on a single topic or main idea in order to produce an effective piece of writing. But finding a focus means more than just knowing what to photograph or write about. Good photographers also think about what they want their photograph to communicate. This affects their decisions about how to frame their subject in the shot, and whether to zoom in for a close-up or zoom out for a wide angle shot. Similarly, writers must think about what they want their topic to communicate.

How to find an angle

1. Combine a topic with a news angle: For example, tik addiction is a topic. Combine it with a news peg it can become a feature.

For example,

a/ Impact of Tik Addiction – a bit vague, needs a tighter angle, the impact on whom?

b/ Relevance - How Tik Addiction Affects You.

c/ Proximity - A recent billboard campaign in Cape Town showed the mayor Patricia de Lille, saying "I have a drug problem." This was a clever ways of conveying that Tik addiction affects us all through escalating crime etc. A possible feature could ask some of those featured on the billboards how tik has affected them.

d/ Prominence - It might be possible to approach celebrities and discover their personal experiences with Tik addiction.

e/ Timeliness - The release of the movie, Four Corners would have provided an opportunity to write a feature around the issue of Tik addiction. For example, a Q&A with one of the gangsters about their experience with Tik.

2. Combine your topic with different types of features:
   For example, an information feature: Is Your Friend on Tik? How to spot the signs of Tik Use.

A first person account: How I escaped Tik addiction.

A general feature: Tik: The devils drug – how Tik radically and permanently affects brain structure.

3. Join two subjects together

Putting together two subjects can give a topic an angle. By itself, crime is a topic. Put it together with another subject and you start to get a story angle. For example, crime and prostitution (should prostitution be criminalized?), crime and prison (Do prisons breed career criminals?)

TASK.

List five topics that interest you.

Write them the top of a single page.

Spend ten minutes jotting down subjects that occur to you. Don't think it through. Just write what comes to find. For example, take the topic health.

Subjects that occur to me are

Smoothies

Vitamins

Exercise

Super foods,

Veganism

Etc.

Now go through your list and join the subjects together and you will get ideas like

Health + smoothies = healthy smoothies for breakfast. Ten power smoothies to kick start your day.

Health + vitamins = Are vitamins really good for your health?

Health +exercise = could exercise be damaging your health?

Health +veganism= How healthy is veganism?

Formulas

Formulas are fun ways to come up with story ideas. In his book, Writing Feature Articles: A Practical Guide to Methods and Markets, Brendan Hennessy suggests the following formulas for coming up with story ideas.

What your ...tells you about yourself (type of phone, breed of dog, car etc.)

What's the best? (Investment policy, medical Aid, degree to study)

The ...of the future (job, phone, food)

Behind the scenes at ...

How to...

Make the most of your...

What makes a... (Great friend, happy home, great soup)

The world's biggest

The world's smallest...

The art of...

Why you should...

Can...Survive? (Banks, print journalism, marriage)

The truth about...

Coping with... (Being single, moving home etc.)

Recovering from...

TASK: Using the formula above, spend 30 minutes filling in the blanks. Come up with 5 suggestions for each formula.

Read over your suggestions and choose three that strike you as good ideas.

TASK: List features

The best

The oldest

The most exciting

The most dangerous

The healthiest

The hardest

Play around with matching topics to these descriptors. Spend five minutes making a list of things that vaguely interest you – cocktails, notebooks, facial etc. Combine these with the list item

For example, the best cocktail – there's an idea! Maybe a feature in which local or well-known figures and celebrities (depending on which publication you are writing for) share their favourite cocktail recipe.

The oldest cocktail – maybe an article on the history of the cocktail – or maybe a side-bar to another feature.

The most exciting...not really

The most dangerous... again, not for me

The healthiest...ah, alcohol free cocktails or how about super-cocktails – combining super foods with alcohol – there's something to explore...

Dictionary doodling

This is great fun.

Write down a subject. Let's say vegetarianism.

Then open the dictionary at random and jot down ten words that catch your eye.

Here's the first two words that I got.

Intimate

Fast

Match the subject and words, let your mind play with the combinations and see what you come up with...

Intimate vegetarianism ...mmm...Can vegetables improve your sex life?

Fast vegetarianism ...five vegetarian meals you can make in less than fifteen minutes

Or a vegetable juice fast.

See how it works...go ahead!

The story viability test

Once you have a good idea for a story you need to sell it to an editor, or pitch it. One of the snags of feature writing is that editors want to see in your pitch where your story will go and what conclusions it will draw. This means that you have to have put a lot of effort into the story before pitching it. Time is money for a feature writer, and writing a good query letter is time consuming, so you want to make sure that you write as many of the ideas as you pitch as possible.

Katherine C. McAdams, Jan Johnson Elliott in A Guide to Media Writing suggests that before you pitch an idea to an editor you must be able to answer "yes" to the following five questions:

1.   Is my topic of interest to the readers of this particular publication?

2.   Is the topic of interest to me? Your best writing will tend to be about topics that interest you. As a young reporter you may be assigned stories that you don't like, but when you are proposing to write feature stories it makes sense to suggest stories that excite you.

3.   Is my topic broad enough and narrow enough? An article on designer handbags is too broad and an article about a single designer handbag (unless it is used by a prominent person) is equally uninteresting.

4.   Are high quality sources of information about my topic available?

5.　　Is my topic of value? All features should be able to answer the reader's question, "What's in it for me?" Readers must be convinced that the article is worth their time. The last response you want from a reader is, "So what?"

If you answer "yes" to all of the above questions, then it's time to sell your idea.

HOW MAGAZINES WORK

"In order to write for magazines, you have to know what they are, who they cater to, and why they exist.

Magazines are about fantasy. They play to the lives we want to led, not necessarily to the lives we do lead. People read Martha Stewart's magazine because they want to be Martha Stewart, and they read *O* because they want to be Oprah Winfrey...

If as a writer you know this about people and can understand their relationship to magazines, you've taken the first step in learning how to write for them.

Any aspiring magazine writer must know the market. Knowing the market means knowing what magazines are out there – and there are plenty of them, for all kinds of interests and tastes- and, perhaps most important, who reads them."

Charles Salzberg, *The Portable MFA in Creative Writing*

Once you have come up with an idea for a feature story you need to match it with an appropriate publication. This means a little analysis.

TASK: Find a bookshop that doesn't mind you browsing through the magazine stand, or a library.

Choose 5 magazines that you would like to focus on writing for.

Who is featured on the cover? Are they under twenty, male or female, or perhaps a couple?

What do the cover lines say? Cover lines are the advertisements for the content inside. For example: Stop sneezing now! A guide to spring allergies.

Watch your waist. Why belly fat is the most important to lose

Feel good at any age.

The 3 cover lines of this fictional publication already give us a clear demographic of its readers'. It's definitely for older women (Feel good at any age) as would undoubtedly be confirmed by the age of the model on the cover. Magazines for older woman tend to picture women who look remarkably young and well-kept for their age.

Now fill in the demographics for 5 magazines that you would like to write for.

AGE:

SEX:

INTERESTS:

CONCERNS:

INCOME LEVEL:

ASPIRATIONS:

Editors and advertisers want articles that appeal to the demographics of their magazine. It's really not worth try to sell a health article to a bikers' magazine or an article about finding your first job to a magazine aimed at mature women.

Finding an outlet for your idea

After you have decided which publication is the best match for your idea the next step is to try and sell your idea to the appropriate editor of that publication. It's time to write what is called a query letter. The query letter is an attempt to persuade the editor that you have an idea for a story that will appeal to their readers and advertisers. You also need to convince the editor that you are skilled enough to write the proposed feature. Editors are wary of commissioning new writers, not because they are mean and nasty, but because it is a risk.

The reason for this is simple. If you examine your favourite publication you will notice that each month the structure is the same. Every magazine has a design template, which is a little like an architectural plan for a house. Each day, week or month the editorial team meets to decide, in advance, the content of the next edition. The design template of the magazine is known as the flat plan. The flat plan specifies the type of content in the magazine and the order in which it occurs.

This is unique for each publication.

For example Fair Lady's Special Report does not occur in every issue and GQ generally does not include human interest features.

In the editorial meeting, specific editors will assign features to their specific departments. For example, the beauty editor will decide to feature mascara in the upcoming issue.

Features are usually assigned by the feature editor.

Often a magazine will be structured around a particular theme. For example, *O* is usually themed around a seasonally appropriate attribute, for example, generosity at Christmas. It creates a crisis if the feature editor commissions a writer who fails to produce a usable article on deadline. In that case, the editor has to pay the writer a "kill fee" and quickly try to fill the space. It's not a situation that editors like to find themselves in. It's not surprising then that editors like to stick to tried and tested writers. And yet, they also want fresh voices and original writing.

That's why you need to write a winning query letter that will persuade the editorial team that you have the ability to write a great story that is suitable for their readers'.

While seasoned writers can afford to write sketchier query letters, beginning writers need to write an outstanding query letter as it's the first impression that you make on the editor. Editors get hundreds of query letters a month, most badly written. Learning how to write a well-structured and written query letter is vital. If you can't write a query letter, it goes to follow that you can't write a feature. Think of your query letter as a sample of your writing.

THE QUERY LETTER

The best query letters display your writing talent. Start the query as you would the article, using a possible lede and assuring the editor that you are a professional who knows that a good feature starts with a good lede.

Structure of the query letter

Query letters should contain the following:

The lede. Use a lede that is appropriate to the tone and type of article that you are writing, preferably a creative lede that uses anecdote, description or dialogue.

A summary sentence, or nut graf, outlining what your story is about and why readers should care about it.

The content. Outline the ideas you will include in the body of the article. Include possible sub-headings.

Specifics. Include the latest facts, statistics and research. Let the editor know who you will interview.

Point of view. Let the editor know your stance on the issue and how you will balance it by including opposite opinions.

Your credentials. Let the editor know why you are qualified to write about this subject.

The type of feature. (First person account, how-to etc.) and why it is suitable for the publication that you are pitching to.

Rules for writing query letters

Query letters must be well written. Editors often pay more attention to your query letter than your clippings. Your published writing has already been through a rigorous editing process and doesn't necessarily reflect your ability as a writer. If your query letter contains grammatical mistakes and bad English usage you will not get the assignment. A good query letter is time consuming to write. But there is no short cut.

Be factually correct. You need to prove to the editor that you can be relied on to provide up-to-date, factually correct information.

Send the query letter to the right editor. Your query letter won't be considered if you send it to the wrong editor in the wrong department. Check the masthead of the magazine and you will find which editors deal with what sections. If you don't find the information that you need from the masthead, call the magazine, ask for the editorial department, and ask who would handle the kind of article you are pitching, for example a profile feature.

Get the editor's name right. If you can't accurately research the correct name and title of the editor that you are addressing, how can you be relied on to write a complex article that quotes experts, gives advice etc.?

Keep focused. Query letters must propose a story with a clearly defined angle. Query letters mustn't ramble. A rambling query letter indicates a rambling writer, a no-no for magazines that value concise, clear and confident writing.

Write in a tone appropriate to the article. If you are propping to write a funny column, display your wit in the query letter. If you are writing about a sensitive issue, let your compassion come through in your writing.

Include all essential information. Don't make the mistake of thinking that you need to withhold your best information, anecdotes and quotes from the editor. Don't tell the editor that you have great information; show that information in your query letter.

Write in the style of the magazine to which you are pitching. A successful feature writer is a chameleon and able to assume the style of whatever publication they are writing for. You need to let the editor know in your query letter that you can adopt the style of their publication.

Send the query as an attachment and pasted in the body of the mail. Some magazines and editors have a hard and fast rule about not opening attachments ever. Side step this by attaching the query and pasting it to the body of the mail.

Following up on the query letter.

You write a well structured query letter with what you think is a brilliant idea. You press send, notice that the whole time you've been writing your query letter your shoulders are attached to your ear lobes, you exhale, drop your shoulders, crack your finger joints and wait for the phone to ring or mail to ping. Nothing happens. You check if the mail did in fact send. Yup. So, what next?

First, remember how magazines work. The features editor might well have received your query, thought it was a good idea and is planning to pitch it at the next editorial meeting.

Most query pitches, if they are going anywhere, will get an answer within two or three weeks. If you haven't got a response within a few weeks from the appropriate editor, send a further email asking if she received it. Query letters do sometimes fall between the cracks and get ignored among the avalanche of mails that feature editors receive. If you don't get a response second time around, give up and look for another publication to pitch to. Depending on your persistence and conviction that this is the right story for this particular publication, you might want to send another mail a few weeks later.

CHAPTER 4: REPORTING

"If ideas are the seeds of stories, then reporting is the fertilizer, the compost of facts, statistics, quotes, interpretations that allows the reporter to produce a factual, complete, clear and accurate story."

Writer and commentator, Chris Scanlan.

All features, except perhaps columns, rely on reporting. Reporting is in essence finding out what you need to know to write with authority. Writing that reads effortlessly often is built on days, weeks, months of reporting. And reporting can be arduous, even dangerous. How much reporting you will be able and willing to do depends on how much the story matters to you and how much you are being paid. Writers have gone to extreme lengths to tell their story. One writer reporting on prisons got himself employed as a prison warder. As a novice writer it is good to be aware of the depth of reporting that goes into the kind of quality journalism we read in high end magazines like Vanity Fair.

One of the biggest problems with students is one of effort. Both in reporting and writing they do the bare minimum. Without solid reporting your stories will lack substance, anecdote and authority. You won't have enough material to weed through to get the juicy stuff.

I suspect that part of the problem is shifting perspective. When you are reporting you are intensely alert, keeping your mind on the writing process, looking for snappy quotes to use, thinking of possible ledes. Developing this kind of detachment is difficult and needs practice. Writing features will change the way you interact with the world. One student, given the task of writing a feature about a local arts event, lamented that she couldn't enjoy it because she was so busy reporting on it. When you are writing about an event, or conducting an interview, you can no longer get swept up in the conversation or experience.

Reporting is detective work

Reporting is both a practical act and a state of mind. In the field, having researched your topic thoroughly, you need to take notes. Psychologically you need to be focused and on high alert. All your senses need to be switched on and you need to suspend your concerns with what you are going to eat for dinner, or where you will take your next vacation, as you immerse yourself in your quest. The length of time that you need to sustain this focus depends on the type of feature that you are writing. Easy features are a quick sprint of a few hours effort. Longer features are a marathon of effort and require training to achieve the necessary endurance.

Collecting information

Journalists use 3 main sources for gathering information:

Documents

Interviews

First hand observation

They use the same sources for news and features, although features require a greater range and depth of material.

While reporting, journalists are collecting the following:

Facts – these are the bedrock of journalism.

Anecdotes – these are mini stories that can be sad, funny, awe inspiring etc.

Quotes – these are effective because they report people in their own voice. Reporting dialogue is doubly effective because it allows readers to hear the actual interplay between people.

Atmosphere - feature stories convey emotions through description, whether of people, events or by quoting dialogue.

Telling details –details are everywhere, but few tell you much. A telling detail is the kind that George Orwell noticed when he was researching life in the mining town of Wigan. He found that miners' pay cheques carried a stamp marked "death stoppage, "meaning a shilling had been deducted to contribute to a fund for fellow miners' widows. The significant detail is the rubber stamp. The rate of accidents is so high that casualties are taken for granted.

Drawing up a reporting plan

 Reporting is time consuming. Interviewing is often exhausting. You have to listen to many hours of rambling discussion before you get what you need. There is definitely room for meandering and taking the road less travelled when reporting a long, well paid commission. But if you have a tight deadline and skinny budget you will need a tight focus.

It's incredibly easy to get lost in a maze of reporting. Once you start researching a topic a thousand side roads and diversions beckon. Whilst they may yield interesting information, you might equally find yourself side-tracked and with a deadline looming. As writing coach Chip Scanlan says, "Generals wouldn't go into battle without a plan. Builders wouldn't lay a foundation without a blue-print in hand. Yet, planning news stories, organizing information into coherent, appropriate structures, is an overlooked activity for all too many journalists."

The Reporting plan

Journalism Coach, Nora Paul suggests that you ask yourself the following questions to help you draw up a reporting plan.

Who?

Who might have the information you need? Who has done the types of research that might advise you?

What?

What information do you already have? What holes do you need to fill? What type of information do you need? Facts? Statistics? Sources? Background information?

When?

When do you need the information? When is your deadline?

Where?

Where might there be coverage of the event/person you are writing about?

Why?

Why do you need the information? Are you fishing or fact checking?

How?

How much information do you need: Just a few anecdotes or in-depth reportage?

RESEARCH

How much information do you need?

Features writers either fall on either side of the reporting fence. On the one side sits the research enthusiast who over researches the topic. By the end of researching for a 2 000 word article they know so much about the topic they deserve a PHD. The problem is that they get so lost in information that they find the writing process impossibly difficult. There is nothing guaranteed to paralyze a writer more as much as information overload. Also, if you explore every nuance of a topic you often lose its essence.

On the other side of the fence sits the feature writer who loves writing and reporting but has little patience for research. His problem is accuracy. In his hurry to interview his sources and write his feature, his main source, a known tax evader, has wrapped him around his little finger. A little research would have revealed the unreliability of this source.

Research is a key to producing a good article. Only you can decide how much research you need to conduct. While people typically provide most of the information for feature stories, documents and background research to the story are important.

Where to research

The internet. This is the obvious and easiest starting point. The search engine Google has revolutionized journalism. But don't neglect other sites for research:

www.expertclick.com

www.profnet.com

www.allexperts.com - This is an amazing service that I use often. You can ask experts, who volunteer their time, specific questions. Often when you are researching you will need a specific answer to a question.

Individual websites. Nowadays, nearly all government agencies have websites where you can quickly and easily retrieve information.

LexisNexis is an online service that has a comprehensive databank of articles from many major publications. It's an amazing resource, but it's expensive and hence often out of reach for students.

Perhaps you can persuade your college to register.

The library. Despite its accessibility, the internet is fraught with inaccuracy. Serious writers must use the library. As old fashioned as it might seem to the Y generation, the library (and librarian) are a reporters best friend.

In the library you will find encyclopaedic lists for every subject imaginable. As well as the obvious The Readers Guide to Periodical Literature you find listings for people who collect bottles and every other imaginable memorabilia.

The white and yellow pages. These are obvious and neglected research tools. Apart from helping you track down people, telephone directories help you verify names and addresses.

Corporate communications and public relations departments. These offices and spokespeople set up interviews and give information. Remember that their job is to maintain a good corporate image, so they are not good sources for quotes and everything that they say needs to be double checked. However, the public relations department is a good start when you are looking for contact details and also if you want to get the corporate side of any issue.

Friends and family. Use the power of six degrees of separation. When you get an assignment tell everyone what you are writing about and ask them if there is anyone that they think you should speak to. Even better is if they can help set up an interview. People enjoy helping others and you will be amazed at the amount of help you can get from friends and colleagues. Often if someone close to a source asks for an interview they will be more inclined to say yes than if they are contacted by you, a stranger.

TASK: You have been tasked to write an article called, "Lucky Winners" for national women's magazine about three women who won a dream vacation in a magazine completion. The women have to have entered the prize – it could not be some kind of lucky draw and they had to win by chance, not merit. In other words, not for writing a prize winning letter.

(The women must live in your country and if America, Not New York or Los Angeles.)

How would you set about finding these three women?

SOURCES

"If you tell students one thing, tell them how incredibly important sources are. You have to develop them – take them to lunch, call them – even when you aren't working on a story."

Tim Belnap Court reporter Detroit Free press

A source is anyone a reporter interviews for a story. The feature writer, just as much as the news reporter relies on sources for both story ideas and story content. Before you choose your sources, you need to evaluate them based on the following questions:

What is the point of the story and can they add value to it?

What is the deadline and are they available in the allotted time?

What is the most appropriate channel to use to interview them – e-mail, telephone or in person?

What background information do I need on the source?

What questions would I ask them and do they serve the story?

REPORTING TIPS

Be relentless

It can take ten calls just to track down a source whose comments may be boiled down to a single quote.

Know when to back off

Being persistent is not the same as invading privacy. If you are asked to stop telephoning, or e-mailing, do so. There's a line between tenacity and intimidation. Don't cross it.

Be friendly

It's simply good practice to be friendly, at all times, to all people. This does not make you a doormat. If someone abuses you or disrespects your boundaries, call their tune. However, cultivating a practice of being friendly is not only good for those around you; it's good for your writing career. You never know when the security guard will become your source. Or whether the cleaner has an epic story to tell. Arrogance is the wrong attitude for any feature writer as you depend on people sharing with you to get your stories written. Keep humble.

Get the secretary on your side

Receptionists and secretaries have a lot of power as the gatekeepers to busy, important people. Get them on your side and they will move mountains. Piss them off and they will make your job much more difficult. Always be polite. Remember, they owe you nothing. Show appreciation for their efforts and thank them for any assistance. A good relationship with a secretary can make a huge difference. They can slip into a meeting to deliver a message or let you know at which hotel the boss is staying. If you can't get the secretary on your side, try calling before 9am, during lunch or after 5pm, times that they might not be manning the phones.

Be forceful

If an important source consistently refuses to speak to you, you can let them know that the story will run with or without their input. Suggest that by granting you an interview they have the opportunity to put forward their side of the story.

Be connected

Feature writers' should spread a wide net of contacts and befriend as many people as possible.

Be diverse

The wonderful thing about journalism is that it gives you a chance to talk to all kinds of people. Reporters should have sources from various political persuasions and from a wide range of ethnic, religious and economic backgrounds.

No law requires anyone to talk to a reporter. But most people will talk, for the following reasons:

Publicity/self-promotion

Revenge

Because they believe the public has a right to know

Sources are especially valuable when they are willing to tell secrets. But what if these secrets would cost the source his job or marriage?

Journalists have developed a series of ground rules for their confidential dealings with sources.

On the record

Reporters should expect the people they interview to attach their names to what they say. When people say things on the record their statements take on greater credibility. People are more likely to be honest when they can be held accountable for what they said.

Not for attribution

While the source may not be identified by name, the reporter may use some non-specific description that gives readers a sense of the source's position without giving away who the source is.

For example:

"A city hall official…"

"A source close to the mayor…"

"An official…"

Reporters press for permission to use the clearest attribution possible. Be as specific as the source allows.

"A high-ranking official" carries more weight than "An official."

Deep background

Sources who provide information on deep background will allow reporters to use information but without any attribution.

Reporters are wary of this for good reason. For example, it allows officials to test policies without taking any responsibility for them.

Off the record

If a source says that information is off the record, ask what they mean. Usually sources mean it is deep background.

Material that is really off the record can't be used at all.

When reporters receive off the record confidences they should honour this in conversation as well as writing.

INTERVIEWING

"Here's a little secret about journalists and interviewing, something you will rarely hear in a classroom: No matter how long you've done it, no matter how many interviews you've conducted, your still going to be nervous before (and maybe during) your next interview. And maybe that's a good thing, because it keeps you on your toes, it keeps you thinking about the interview, and it gets the adrenalin going."

Charles Salzberg in *The Portable MFA in Creative Writing*.

No matter how awkward you may feel at the prospect of asking strangers questions, as a feature writer it is something that you will have to do regularly. There's simply no getting round it. Interviews are essential for features. They are where we get material for writing stories. Without people and quotes, there is no story. The people that you choose to interview, as well as the way that you interview them, will influence the focus, angle and even the structure of your story. The best way to deal with the nerves that will inevitably plague you as you begin an interview is to be well prepared.

Asses your subject

You should have already have made these decisions at the research stage and when you drew up your reporting plan, but just to recap:

Is this the best possible person to talk on this subject/in this field?

Is the person available? Will they be able to schedule an interview before your deadline?

Is this person willing to go on record?

If the source wants to be anonymous, how will that affect the story? Will your editor accept this?

Why is this person agreeing to the interview? Could there be any ulterior motives (publicity; vindication; revenge; political grandstanding etc). If so, will that hinder the story?

The interviewing process

Requesting an interview

You don't just phone someone up and launch into questions, or appear on their doorstep with a notepad in hand. Rather, you contact them initially and request an interview. After introducing yourself, explain what the story is about and why you are writing it. Explain what you feel that they can contribute to the story.

Ask for the amount of time that you think the interview will take. Be honest about this. Don't ask for fifteen minutes of their time if you are planning an in-depth interview. And don't be unreasonable. No-one wants will agree to several hours of questioning. If you need to cover a lot of material, it's better to interview in stages, so that you don't exhaust your subjects. You are not conducting an FBI interrogation.

Pre-Interview research

There is a direct relationship between what you know before an interview and what you can find out during it. If, for example, your do not know that your subject, the Financial Minister, had a brief stint as a businessman during which time he owned a notorious nightclub, you won't know to broach this subject in the interview.

Feature writers who go to interview an author about the latest book they have written and don't read it, should find another profession. Ensure that before interviewing a politician, you understand their politics and before interviewing the company executive, you understand the major developments in their business. While you should be open to learning during the interview, you should be clear of the facts beforehand.

You should also know what your goal is in the interview. Novice feature writers should devote considerable thought to what they are trying to accomplish in an interview and how best to accomplish it.

If you want subjective comments, you should ask questions like: What was it like? What were you feeling at the time? How did you react? What would you compare this experience to? If, however your goal is analysis, most of your questions should use the words, Explain, Interpret, Predict and Analyse.

Research allows you to get past the initial 'surface' questions on an issue. If you are interviewing an expert, read any research papers they have published. Read reports and articles written by other experts and commentators on the issue that you will be interviewing your subject about.

Jot down a list of questions as guidelines

Good interviewers are always open to new avenues of questioning should they present themselves. However, a list of questions serves to keep the interview on track and helps you regain your ground if you momentarily lose your way. As you jot down your questions, try to anticipate possible answers so that you can envision the possible flow of the interview. Start with basic who, what, when, where why and how of the subject to establish that you have got your facts right.

The number of questions that you prepare depends on the complexity of the issue that you are exploring and the word count of the article you are writing.

Conducting the interview

Establish a connection. Try and make a physical connection by shaking hands, but keep your boundaries. You are not trying to make friends. No hugs or kisses.

Pay attention to your appearance. Consider matching your appearance to that of the person you will be interviewing. For example, a surfer might feel more comfortable if you are dressed informally, while a corporate executive might feel that you are unprofessional if you come to an interview wearing jeans and sneakers.

Start the interview with open ended questions. There is no such thing as a dull interview, only dull questions. Get the conversation rolling by asking questions like, "Tell me about …", "How did you feel …", "What do you think about". One incredibly useful phrase is "Can you tell me more about that."

Listen. My first piece of advice to inexperienced interviewers is: Listen to the answers. This might seem obvious but so often novice writers and reporters have so much on their mind that they forget to listen to the answers to their questions.

Work on your flow. Try to make the interview seem like a conversation - arrange the questions so that they flow logically.

Ask closed questions. These are questions that require either a yes, or no, answer. In the search for facts, or confirmation of facts, closed questions are the best option.

Get specifics. An anecdote usually makes a point better than a statement. Say, for example, that you are interviewing a top earning model who is also a student and she says that her work and studies sometimes clash, ask her to recall a specific incident when the two aspects of her life collided. Then she will give you a valuable anecdote, something like, "One day the shoot lasted until 10pm. Everyone else goes home to sleep but I had to stay up all night swotting for a test next day."

Be yourself. Don't create a persona that's not you. Don't think that you have to be aggressive or unrelenting. If you are shy or nervous, don't worry. The interviewee is far too worried about how they are coming across to notice your nerves. If you are naturally shy, that can work to your advantage. Sometimes aggressive A type personalities come on too strong and dominate conversations. Shy people make good listeners and often the best interviewers.

Here's a few words of encouragement from master teacher, William Zinsser: "Interviewing is one of those skills you can only get better at. You will never again feel so ill at ease as when you try it for the first time, and probably you'll never feel entirely comfortable prodding another person for answers he or she may be too shy or too inarticulate to reveal. But much of the skill is mechanical. The rest is instinct – knowing how to make the other person relax, when to push, when to listen, when to stop. This can all be learned with experience."

Pace yourself. Everyone operates at a different speed. Task driven people will tend to talk faster and get to the point quickly. You might have to speed up when interviewing them or they might get frustrated. On the other hand, people orientated people may want to form a connection first. Take time to find the comfortable pace of the person you are interviewing and match it as far as possible.

Manage the time. If you sense the interviewee is in a hurry, adjust your timing accordingly. If they seem too busy to talk don't try to persevere. Rather say, "I can sense that you are busy. Would you like to reschedule." Trying to conduct an interview in the midst of an unexpected crisis is a waste of time.

Standard interview time can be anything between 20 minutes to 3 hours, but make sure that you stick to the time you agreed upon when you made the appointment. Often people will run over time. If so, say something to the effect of "I notice that we're about to run over our scheduled time. Are you fine to continue?" People will feel that you are in control and be willing and able to relax.

Give yourself plenty of time between appointments to avoid scheduling conflicts. Do not book interviews back to back but always leave a couple of hours between in case you interview is going well. The last thing you want is to have to jump up and leave just when your interviewee is revealing the juicy stuff.

Observe everything. Add colour by taking in your surroundings. Details about the room, your subject's mannerisms, all add colour to the story.

 Conduct your interview in your subject's personal space. This will tell you more about your subject. You will be able to observe the pictures on their walls and how they interact with those they share their space with. Avoid neutral venues like coffee shops, as they don't provide any insight into your subject.

Interrupt when you don't understand. Don't just nod your head and feign understanding. If you don't understand something that your interviewee says during the interview it won't become any clearer when you are at home at your desk. Keep your audience in mind. One reason you are conducting this interview is to explain an issue or get behind a trend. Ask for explanations

If your subject uses scientific jargon or explanations you don't understand, politely interrupt and ask for further explanation. Play dumb. Never be embarrassed about not knowing something. When I was writing a story about Ithemba nuclear physics labs, I found it impossible to understand what the scientists were doing there, despite their best efforts to explain it. Eventually I asked one scientist if he had children. He said he had a six year old. I said ok, now can you explain what you do here as though were explaining it to her. The result was magic.

Keep quiet. When you start asking provocative or personal questions, the answers most likely will be short, useless or carefully worded. You may not get an answer at all. If this occurs, look your source in the eye and say nothing. "I'm not afraid to shut up and let sources fill in the silence," Says Tom French of the St. Petersburg Times.

Don't debate. If you disagree with the interviewee, hold your tongue. You are there to get his opinion, not set forth your own.

Be aware of your body language. Eye contact, head nodding and leaning forward are encouraging gestures that you can use to help the person you are interviewing open up.

On the other hand, darting eyes send a signal that you are distracted or bored which can make the interviewee reluctant to talk.

Maintain eye contact. A reporter who spends most of the interview bent over taking notes or looking into a notebook can be disconcerting. Learn to take abbreviated notes looking down only once in a while so you can focus on your interviewee. This will make the interview more like a conversation, and enable everyone to be more relaxed.

Ask for what you need. Try to anticipate the writing process. Don't be afraid to tell the interviewee what you need. You can say, "Listen, I really need a quote from you encapsulating your feelings on this issue," or "I want to make sure I've got the chronology of events clear."

End tough. As the interview is drawing to a close, ask those awkward questions, even if by now you feel you are the interviewee's new best friend, don't lose sight of your purpose (or your values – right to know, remember). By the end of an interview you have less to lose by alienating subjects and additionally, after a long interview, they might be more inclined to let down their guard.

Useful questions that should be on the tip of every aspiring interviewers tongue:

Could you be more specific?

Could you give me an example of that?

Can you describe exactly what it was like?

Can you remember exactly what happened?

Can you recall a specific incident?

Before you leave...

Always ask your interviewee, "Do you have anything to add?" "Is there anything else I should have asked" Or "Is there anyone else you can suggest I speak to." Always ask for other sources. Colleagues or friends of the interviewee may be more knowledgeable or willing and able to speak to you.

Always leave your business card in case they think of anything else they would like to add.

Warn them that you might have follow-up questions and get their contact details.

Thank them for their time and write a follow-up email thanking them again.

Getting people to talk

Contrary to what beginner interviewers believe, the biggest problem in interviews is not getting people to talk, it's to get them to stop talking. Do not let your subject derail the interview and get onto his pet topic. Politely but firmly bring him back to the topic, saying something like "That's really interesting, but there's still a lot I want to know about..."

Also, some people are lonely and having someone listen to them intently is something that they crave. Be aware. Some of your subjects will fall in love with you (and sharply out of love once they read a less than idealized portrayal of them).

Some subjects will hijack you and want to talk for hours. Unless you are writing an intimate story about a sensitive subject, it might be time to leave when they haul out the family photo album.

Asking difficult questions

Whatever interviewing technique you choose to use, a golden rule is never to ask difficult questions or make accusations at the start of the interview.

Don't hit the interviewee with awkward questions first. Help your subject relax by initially asking them non-threatening questions about a topic that makes them feel good – their golf handicap, for example.

Be aware that the act of humble enquiry is often more effective than accusation. Let's imagine that you are interviewing a Minister of Education who supports slashing the education budget. In such an instance, confrontational questions, such as "How can you talk of improving education when you have slashed expenditure on the education portfolio?" are guaranteed to be met with silence.

Try instead: "What are your suggestions for improving education."

This will give your subject room to manoeuvre; they will relax, see this an easy publicity interview and be more forthcoming.

Don't let them off the hook, though. Remember, talk is cheap.

Follow the humble question with a tougher one, for example:

"What measures have you implemented to achieve these improvements?"

Presumably the minister will have enough up their sleeve to attempt to fob you off.

Now is the time to confront them with the damming information that you have. Having vigorously researched your topic, you already know that they have voted to slash the education budget. You have given them the illusion of control, but you have been in control all along.

Is it not true that on June 10th you voted to slash expenditure on the education portfolio by 10%?

In Interviews that Work, Shirley Biagi describes two effective interview strategies:

The funnel interview

This is largely similar to the approach outlined above and is used to back a newsmaker into a corner. Biagi uses an example of a police officer alleged to have beaten a subject. The reporter opens with general questions about suspects and the proper way to treat them and gets increasingly specific about what is alleged to have happened until they ask a question that can't be evaded, such as "Then how can you justify the rough handling that someone obviously gave that murderer."

Covertly Sequenced Interview

 This is a technique that involves spreading trickier questions throughout the interview to surprise the newsmaker or lead the newsmaker into contradictions. For example, the reporter might ask early on whether the officer has known of any police officers who have used physical force with a suspect in custody, then after some innocuous questions, ask whether the officer himself has ever felt a desire or need to use physical force with a suspect in custody. Then after another interval of harmless questioning, ask about how he treated the accused murderer.

Machine gun interview

After an amicable start to the interview ask a series of tough questions, posed rapidly, that leave little room for evasion: Were you ever in a room alone with the suspect. Did you hit him? Did he make you angry?

Whichever technique you use will depend on the person and the situation. If the person you are interviewing threatens to walk out it's not time to use the rapid question machine gun approach. But if they are confident and evasive, such a direct approach might be your best option.

Follow up

Most people will be impressed rather than annoyed by a diligent reporter who calls back to clarify points.

Many interviewees will request that they see the copy before it goes to print. Politely refuse. You will avoid the potential nightmare of a source wanting to dictate what you write. You are not a publicity agent and you don't want to be held to ransom before deadline by a source who quibbles with what you have written or goes overseas before they return the copy. Very often, when sources see their statements in print they will want to retract them.

When newsmakers ask if they can approve copy before publication, I explain to them that, I'm sorry, but it is against our publication's media policy to show sources finished articles. Reporters should never surrender final control of an article to sources by letting them read a final manuscript before publication.

If they become insistent I have on occasion suggested that I read them excerpts over the phone.

Post-interview

Immediately after the interview collect your thoughts and write up your notes. Resist the urge to debrief in the pub with friends. Interviews are intense and it's often tempting to socialize as a let-down. This is not a good idea. You will lose valuable ideas, threads, memories and impressions. Remember the interview means nothing until you have written the story.

Be disciplined and type up your notes as soon as you get home. Many of your notes will inevitably be garbled and typing them up immediately after an interview gives you the best chance of remembering accurately what was said. Typing notes strait away will help you with the writing. During the interview you will have ideas about quotes to use and possible ledes. You will find that as you type up your notes you will get ideas about story structure.

Note taking

Taking notes is an odious part of the feature writer's job. While students prefer to take screen shots of lectures and save power points, I force them to take notes during lectures as they need to practice this skill: when they go out into the field they cannot avoid taking notes. Some tell me that they will video the interview, but this is intimidating for many subjects and most people, understandably, clam up when you shove a phone in their face.

People being interviewed can talk faster than most reporters can write. It's a pity that shorthand is no longer taught and, like typing, it should be compulsory for all journalists to learn. If you write professionally, knowing how to touch type and take shorthand will earn you weeks of time. Most reporters, by necessity, develop their own form of short hand through practice. Here are a few tips for taking notes:

Only write down what's important

Beginner reporters write down everything; experienced reporters think before they write and write down only what's important.

Slow down the pace by asking irrelevant questions

One trick is if the interviewee has said something significant that you want to get down ask them a throwaway question, such as "I imagine you've had a lot of time away from your family?" While they are answering, you can catch up with your notes.

Recording

Many of my students resist note taking, arguing that they will record the interview. It is my firm opinion that you cannot be a journalist and not take notes. The best approach is to both record and takes notes.

Here's why:

Listening to recordings is slow. Glancing at notes will help you shape and write your story quicker.

Technologies (and people) do malfunction. Guaranteed. One day, and maybe the day that you land that ace assignment, you will arrive back at the office and discover that the pause button was on for the duration of the interview.

Tape recorders pick up back ground sounds and are often unpleasant to listen to. During a conversation you screen out those sounds, but when you listen to the recording the background music, plates scraping and snippets of conversation, all come through loud and clear.

Taking notes keeps you focused. Taking notes has the effect of slowing down the interview; helping you pay attention to what is being said, keeping you present and alert. If you pick up a good quote, you will often have to ask the person you are interviewing to repeat it, so that when you come to write the piece that quote sticks in your mind, giving you a clear direction.

TASK: PRACTICE NOTE TAKING.

Watch the YouTube video journalism 101: The lede.

Take notes.

Now, write an essay on ledes from what you have written.

TASK

Write an 800 word feature based on the following assignment:

1.   Interview the security at a local bookstore about the problem of book theft and its prevention.

2.   Interview a fire department about the problem of false alarms.

Phone interviews

Phone interviews lack the intimacy and nuance of personal interviews. However, occasionally they are unavoidable, for example, if you are interviewing someone in another country.

In that case, the words become even more important and it's a good idea to tape the conversation.

Remember, however, that you must ask permission to tape a phone conversation as in some places it's illegal to tape a phone conversation without permission.

Don't call without warning and begin the interview. Make preliminary contact and establish a suitable time. Tell the source what story you are working on and what kind of information you will want to find out in the interview. No-one wants to be tongue tied in an interview and this will help them think about what they want to say which will help your feature.

Also, agree on a time span: keep it under an hour. No-one, not even the most avid chatter box, wants to spend the whole night on the phone with a journalist.

E-mail interviews

These are the best form of interview for the Q&A. Simply write up a list of clear and concise questions and send them to the subject, clearly requesting that they return the answers by a certain date. Don't ask them to return them by the next day, but don't give them longer than a week, otherwise they will lie around collecting dust.

Apart from the Q&A interview, email interviews are best avoided. You won't get good quotes from email interviews as responses sound stilted – people don't type in the same way as they talk. The answers to your questions will appear dull and considered. The interviewee will edit all flubs, sometimes the most charming part of an interview.

CHAPTER 5: WRITING

"It is vital to remember that form can never determine substance – technique should never alter the facts. The journalist's use of narrative forms must always be governed by the principles of accuracy and truthfulness. Regardless of the form of the presentation, the most engaging thing of all must be kept in mind: The story is true."

Bill Kovach and Tom Rosenstiel in *The Elements of Journalism*

Structuring your story

So you've been commissioned to write the story! Yeah! Terrific you think. Then the dread begins.

Don't panic. By now you already have your lede. You just need to structure your story. I wish I could tell you exactly, step by step, how to write your story. Really I do. But there honestly is no formula. However, there are some hints and tricks. Here are a few classic story structures that journalists use.

The inverted pyramid

This is the structure of writing used in most news reports. It places the most important information at the top of the article, arranging the what, who, where and when of the news in a logical order. The inverted pyramid structure serves the practical purpose of allowing editors to cut stories to fit the space available.

The inverted pyramid is much critiqued for being boring – giving away all the good bits first and not giving the reader any incentive for reading further.

The hour glass or champagne glass

This uses a traditional news lede, and starts out like the inverted pyramid, organizing the what, who, where, when and why of the story in a logical order.

Then, there is a break in the pyramid, and a line that begins a narrative, often chronologically, as in, "The incident began when.." The writer then shifts into more narrative techniques, building character and using dialogue.

Here are a few innovative ways to structure your story:

Focus on the how of the story

Before you dismiss the inverted pyramid entirely, consider that Shakespeare's Romeo and Juliet gives away all the essentials of the story in the first 14 lines, even telling us the ending! As in an inverted pyramid story, the what, who, where and why are all packed into the start of the story.

As Roy Peter Clark writes in How to Write a Good Story in 800 Words or Less: "That's 14 lines, 106 words. Never was there a summary of complex news more carefully crafted or more beautifully expressed. "

Two households, both alike in dignity,

In fair Verona, where we lay our scene,

From ancient grudge break to new mutiny,

Where civil blood makes civil hands unclean.

From forth the fatal loins of these two foes

A pair of star-crossed lovers take their life;

Whose misadventured piteous overthrows

Doth with their death bury their parents' strife.

The fearful passage of their death-marked love,

And the continuance of their parents' rage,

Which, but their children's end, naught could remove,

Is now the two hours' traffic of our stage;

The which if you with patient ears attend,

What here shall miss, our toil shall strive to mend.

After this succinct introduction the remaining two hours are spent on stage answering the question, "How did that happen?"

When you are writing a news orientated feature, consider focusing on the how of the story. Try writing your story in response to the question, how did this happen?

Find the hidden metaphor in your story

ABC News correspondent's Robert Krulwich's method is to find the hidden material in each story that makes it memorable and unique. He often uses surprising and unusual metaphors to help viewers identify with the abstract difficult topics that he covers, explaining currency devaluation in terms of a singing chicken, for example.

Connect your story to deeper themes

News correspondent John Larson describes what he calls the reveal – the hidden surprise that is a key element of good storytelling. He says the best kind of reveal is when a story connects to some deeper unexpected themes. It's when stories "reach us on some elemental level. They talk about a mother's love for her children, a husband's pride in his country. Ambition, avarice, greed. There's something very important that's always going on in a very simple way in good stories."

Use character in your story

Character is a key element in pulling readers into stories. Character is revealed through dialogue, so if possible, let your characters speak in their own words in your feature. Also try to use telling and possibly poignant details to reveal character.

Mix up the chronology

Often the most boring way to tell a story is to start in the beginning and proceed chronologically to the end. What happens if you switch the beginning and the end of your story? Play around and see what happens.

Weave action and commentary

Another approach that can build drama is to withhold the outcome and alternate between chronological events and commentary. This works well with tense situation, such as hostage situations. The reader wants to know the outcome and is held captive to the end.

The writing Process

"No one, not even the greatest writers, creates good first draughts... first draughts might have promising sentences or paragraphs, a brilliant conceptualization, a few surprising turns of phrase, or a sturdy framework. All that, however, will probably be barely visible, entangled in the general messiness of half-formed ideas. Those promising elements will begin to reveal themselves as the writer begins to tease apart the mess with the next draught and the one after that."

Gay Talese

Writing a kind of schizophrenic process that uses two separate and even antagonistic, parts of the brain.

First the artist must create a story out of a mound of reporting. This needs a playful, inspired attitude to allow an enthusiastic rush of ideas to come forth onto the page.

Then, it is time for the critical editor to step in with a red pen. The artist must step aside and let the expert craftsperson cut away the dross.

Often problems with writing occur because novice writers don't understand the two fold nature of the writing process. The artist can't be creative if the critic is looking over their shoulder, muttering "well that's not very good is it." And the writing will be muddled and confused if the artist, satisfied that they done their lot, submits a first draught, puts their feet up and pours a congratulatory whiskey, leaving an irate editor to wade through a muddle of tangled ideas.

If the initial rush of inspiration doesn't come, it's often a problem with the editor interfering with the artist and demanding that you make their job easier by writing correctly, punctuation and all, on your first attempt.

You need to be grateful to your artistic muse and accept that she will make spelling errors while trying to capture the essence of the story.

Accept that your first draught will be flawed, full off errors and ghastly spelling mistakes. Reassure your critic that she will get her chance later.

When you break writing down into two separate tasks – writing and rewriting, it becomes so much easier.

 Students always nod in agreement when I tell them that their first draught will be rubbish and they will have to rewrite their piece several times before it is ready to submit. I emphasize the importance of rewriting. Rewriting, not writing, is the hard part and they must, must, must rewrite. But many secretly don't believe me and submit first draughts.

Don't take my word for it. Here's Gay Talese revealing to Elon Green the agonies that he took with writing his famous Sinatra profile.

The two blondes, who seemed to be in their middle thirties, were preened and polished, their matured bodies softly molded within tight dark suits.

Green: The punctuated alliteration is gorgeous — "preened and polished"; "matured" and "molded". How much time would you spend on such a sentence?

Talese: Oh, I could spend days. Sometimes these phrases come to you and sometimes they're terrible. Sometimes you think, "Maybe that's okay" and you let it in. I throw a lot of stuff away.

Green: What percentage of what you write for any given story do you get rid of?

Talese: More than half. Because it's so easily the case that it's turgid or overwritten.

Green: Do you throw away more now, now that you use a computer?

Talese: I don't think so. I've always thrown a lot away, even when I was working on daily deadlines for newspapers. That was really expensive because at the New York Times we were typing what they called a "book" — it had seven or eight pieces of carbon. A thick thing. If you threw it away, you were destroying 11 cents worth of, well, something.

Writing is a process and you will find writing easier if you break it down into these four steps.

Write a first draught of the story from memory alone. Relying on instinct, ignore your notes. Be creative. Be bold and daring. Write your first thoughts and initial impressions. Try to get a sense of the overall shape of the story. Don't worry about grammar, punctuation or getting the facts right.

Rewrite your garbled first draught, using your notes to fill in any gaps. Pay attention to the logical flow of ideas, checking that one paragraph leads to the next. Correct errors in structure, shifting paragraphs around if necessary. Do a spell check.

Print out your text. Read your text out loud. Listen to the sound of the piece. Does it flow? Do you want to make any changes?

Correct any remaining grammar errors on the hard copy. Read each sentence carefully; interrogate each word.

WRITING THE LEDE

"The most important sentence in any article is the first line. If it doesn't induce the reader to proceed to the second sentence your article is dead. And if the second sentence doesn't induce him to continue to the third sentence, it's equally dead. Of such a progression of sentences, each tugging the reader forward until he is hooked, a writer constructs that fateful unit, "the lede."

William Zinsser, *On Writing Well*

Whereas hard-news ledes need to get all the important points of the story – the who, what, where, when, why and how – into the very first sentence, feature ledes, sometimes called delayed leads, unfold more slowly, drawing the reader into the story, to make them want to read more.

There are many different names and many different types of ledes. As with everything in feature writing, there are not exact formulas. Writing is an art, not a science and cannot be reduced to e=mc2. However, we can identify similar types of ledes that work well with particular stories.

Below are several of the most often used and effective ledes:

Anecdotal Ledes:

An anecdotal lede is a short narrative with a beginning, middle and end. The end is particularly important. It's analogous to the punch line in a joke - it wraps up the story with a flourish that brings things to an apt conclusion.

Here is a terrific example in Kathleen Merryman's profile of palaeontologist Richard Leakey in the Tacoma News Tribune. It's both ironic, odd and explains something central about the subject:

Richard Leakey likes to tell about the day in 1950 when he was a 6-year-old whining for his parents' attention. Louis and Mary Leakey were digging for ancient bones on the shores of Lake Victoria, but their little boy wanted to play. He wanted lunch. He wanted his mother to cuddle him. He wanted something to do.

"Go find your own bone," said his exasperated father, waving Richard off toward scraps of fossils lying around the site.

What the little boy found was the jawbone -- the best ever unearthed -- of an extinct giant pig. As he worked away at it with the dental picks and brushes that served for toys in the palaeontologists' camp, he experienced for the first time the passion of discovery.

Narrative Ledes

A narrative launches into the action of a story, introducing the main characters, the conflict, and perhaps the setting of the story. It makes readers feel the drama and want to know what's going to happen next. Here is a compelling example from Angelo Henderson's Pulitzer Prize winning feature in the Wall Street Journal.

"Get on the ground," a man holding a gun screamed. "I'll blow your heads off if you move."

Dennis Grehl and a co-worker complied. Dreamlike, he found himself lying face down on a cold, gritty black-tile floor, a pistol against the back of his head.

"Please, mister, don't make me shoot you," a second gunman threatened.

A crazy memory: tiny specks of light floating in the tile; that, and the paralyzing weight of helplessness.

Mr. Grehl is a pharmacist, unassuming, mild mannered. A family man with a wife and a daughter.

He was being robbed.

Descriptive/Scene-Setting Ledes:

Feature ledes often begin by setting a scene or painting a picture - in words - of a person or place. These ledes are typically used for stories in which setting is important. The description creates a stage on which the action can unfold and gives a sense of place that is important to the focus of the story.

The story, Mozart in Nyanga, uses a descriptive lede.

The wind whips up dust circles on the streets of Nyanga, Cape Town's oldest township and home to over 10 000 people. People mill and congregate on the streets: a man holds a woman's hand; a mother walks behind her three children wearing brightly colored woolen caps; street vendors grill skewers of cow's intestines over fires in tin drums. Goats saunter down the street.

The surprising sound of a bow being scraped slowly across a violin string accompanies this scene like a musical score to a movie. Follow the sound of Mozart's Twinkle Twinkle Little Star, played with a beginner's halting uncertainty, and you arrive at Hlengisa Primary School. Peer inside the window and you will see a group of six kids, violins tucked neatly under their chins.

Focus Ledes/Single-Instance Ledes/ Microcosm Ledes

The single-instance lede uses one example to illustrate a larger topic. I prefer the term focus ledes as it suggests the way that the writer zooms into a subject like a photographer, then takes a wide angle view in the following paragraph (the nut graf).

This type of lede is also sometimes referred to as the human lede. It works particularly well in the following cases:

To evoke empathy and make readers feel. A statistic such as 7 women are raped every second in South Africa makes us feel nothing. Showing us one instance of a woman suffering the ordeal of rape makes readers identify with the issue.

To illustrate abstract topics. For example, if you are writing a feature about problems with public transport you could start the feature with abstract statistics.

60 percent of students at Omega take public transport to college. 40 percent of trains leave 40 minutes after scheduled time which can explain why so many students are often late for 9am lectures.

Or you could use a focus lede:

Jane arrives out of breath, exhausted and twenty minutes late for her journalism exam. Despite waking up at 5am to ensure that she arrived at the train platform at 6am. The teacher looks at her disapprovingly and

Jane feels tears smart her eyes. She had boarded the train at 6.50. It was crowded and she had to stand. A delay on the track took fifty minutes to resolve. She arrived at the station at 9.05. Late again. And at a critical time.

Then you add the statistics.

It's easy to see that the second approach is better. We identify with Jane's plight and then discover that many other students are facing similar problems in the next paragraph.

A good rule is to start with a person and then broaden the story to include facts and figures. This goes against novice writer's instincts.

Analogy lede.

 This lede makes a comparison between an issue or event and something more familiar to the average reader. This approach can work well when you have a complex or foreign matter you want to explain in laymen's terms. Here's an excellent example by Kevin Kelly in *The Robots*, published in GQ magazine that argues that we embrace, not fear, the rise of robots:

"Imagine that seven out of ten South Africans got fired tomorrow. What would they all do? It's hard to believe you'd have an economy at all if you gave pink slips to more than half the labor force. But that, in slow motion, is what the industrial revolution did to the workforce in the early 19th century. In the United States 200 years ago, 70 percent of workers lived on the farm. Today, automation has replaced all but one percent of their jobs, replacing them (and their work animals) with machines. But the displaced workers did not sit idle. Instead, automation created hundreds of millions of jobs in entirely new fields. Those who once farmed were now manning the legions of factories that churned out farm equipment, cars, and other industrial products. Since then, wave after wave of new occupations have arrived – appliance repairman, offset printer, food chemist, photographer, web designer – each building on previous automation. Today the vast majority of us are doing jobs that no farmer from the 1800's could have imagined."

Less important, more gimmicky ledes include:

Word play ledes: This lede involves a clever turn of phrase, name or word. Essentially light-hearted ledes, word-play ledes therefore work best in entertaining stories and are popular in sports and entertainment features. Obviously, they are unsuited to serious issues.

Amazing fact ledes: Open with an amazing fact that arouses reader's interest, such as the lede I used in a men's health feature in Longevity:

The longevity gap between the sexes is astonishing. In the lucky few who live to be over 100, women outnumber men nine to one. The average man lives a shorter life than the average woman, and for 15 years of that life he can expect to be seriously or chronically ill.

List ledes: Sometimes instead of focusing on just one person, place or thing, you want to impress the reader with a longer list. This can work well for trend features and information features.

Tips for writing the lede

Write your first attempt without using your notes. By now, having researched your topic and reported on it, you have the story in your head. You know the most important points, clever quotes and the amusing anecdotes.

Give the reader a promise which hints what the outcome of the story.

Do not give away the ending. Leave room for an element of surprise. Keep the reader on tender hooks. Identify the conflict and promise that it will be resolved without giving away the resolution

Decide where you want your story to end. Keep the end in view as you write, and use the information and anecdotes that take you most directly to that route.

The nut graf

"A paragraph that says what this whole story is about and why you should read it. It's a flag to the reader, high up in the story: You can decide to proceed or not, but if you read no farther, you know what that story's about."

Ken Wells, writer and editor at *The Wall Street Journal*

The nut graf is where the feature writer lays out for the reader exactly what the story is all about. It usually follows the first few paragraphs of the scene-setting or story-telling the writer has done. A nut graf can be a single paragraph or more that distills the article down to its essence.

The nut graf tells the reader what the writer is up to; it delivers a promise of the story's content and message. It's called the nut graf because, like a nut, it contains the "kernel," or essential theme, of the story. At The Philadelphia Inquirer, reporters and editors called it the "You may have wondered why we invited you to this party?" section.

The lede is often like a close-up that zooms into a single person or event. The nut graf is like a wide-angle shot, showing the isolated incident in a wider context.

The nut graf serves several purposes:

Justifies the story by telling readers why they should care.

Provides a transition from the lead and explains the lead and its connection to the rest of the story.

Tells readers why the story is timely.

It often includes supporting material that helps readers see why the story is important.

William E. Blundell, former Wall Street Journal writer calls the nut graf "the main theme statement the single most important bit of writing I do on any story."

The nut graf used in features replaces the function of the inverted pyramid's summary lead, providing readers with the gist of the story up high, giving the broad outlines of the story and letting them decide if wanted to read further.

In his book, *Follow the Story: How to Write Successful Nonfiction*, James B. Stewart, a former Wall Street Journal front page editor gives the following tips for writing nut grafs:

Never give away the ending of the story. Don't let nut grafs tell the reader so much about the story that they have no incentive to keep reading

Anticipate questions that readers might be asking early in a story, and address them.

Gives readers a concrete reason or reasons to read on.

The young Egyptian professional could pass for any New York bachelor.

Dressed in a crisp polo shirt and swathed in cologne, he races his Nissan Maxima through the rain-slicked streets of Manhattan, late for a date with a tall brunette. At red lights, he fusses with his hair.

What sets the bachelor apart from other young men on the make is the chaperon sitting next to him -- a tall, bearded man in a white robe and stiff embroidered hat.

"I pray that Allah will bring this couple together," the man, Sheik Reda Shata, says, clutching his seat belt and urging the bachelor to slow down.

Christian singles have coffee hour. Young Jews have JDate. But many Muslims believe that it is forbidden for an unmarried man and woman to meet in private. In predominantly Muslim countries, the job of making introductions and even arranging marriages typically falls to a vast network of family and friends.

In Brooklyn, there is Mr. Shata.

Week after week, Muslims embark on dates with him in tow. Mr. Shata, the imam of a Bay Ridge mosque, juggles some 550 "marriage candidates," from a gold-toothed electrician to a professor at Columbia University. The meetings often unfold on the green velour couch of his office, or over a meal at his favorite Yemeni restaurant on Atlantic Avenue.

After a scenic/descriptive lede we find out in the nut graf (In Brooklyn, there is Mr. Shata.

Week after week, Muslims embark on dates with him in tow. Mr. Shata, the imam of a Bay Ridge mosque, juggles some 550 "marriage candidates," ...)

That this is the story of a Brooklyn imam who helps bring young Muslim couples together for marriage.

CHAPTER 6: TIPS FOR WRITING SPECIFIC FEATURES

"Things that I would never tell anyone, you can go down to the bookstore and find out."

Montaigne

The first person account

Yeah! This is when you get the chance to toss down your pen and go bungee jumping, sky-diving or any other activity that you've longed to experience. Participatory pieces are first person accounts where the writer undertakes an interesting experience and lets the reader experience it vicariously. Actually, the best in the genre are not the obvious "look at me having a good time pieces" but more gruelling ordeals, like working in a warehouse, or prison.

Tips:

Choose a good topic: A good topic needs conflict and action. When tasked with writing a first person account one talented student wrote about drinking coffee at a famed coffee spot. The topic was too small. It had no conflict. What could really happen in between ordering the coffee and drinking it? Getting a foam moustache is probably the most exciting thing that could happen and that's not enough to hang a feature on. However, had the student written about serving his first cappuccino in the same establishment then the story could have some drama. There would be some emotion. Presumably the writer would feel daunted by delivering the goods to coffee snobs. Would they manage to get the signature squiggle in the foam? All the better if things go terribly wrong.

Does your topic allow you to emerge as a hero? Readers love reading about you winning against the odds, for example, pouring the perfect cappuccino despite your delirium tremens. So choose topics that will present a challenge. This doesn't have to be obvious. Folding sweaters is not an exciting topic, but I could have made my stint folding sweaters at Benetton work as a first persona feature by showing an impatient, thrill seeking, people orientated character – me – coming up against obsessive, compulsive, object orientated perfectionism in a confined space.

Writing the participatory feature

Go into the activity 'cold' without knowing much about it. That way you will experience things from a fresh perspective and take the reader on a learning journey with you.

Make notes: It is important to write down notes and your thoughts right after participating in the activity while it is fresh in your mind. Doing this will make your recollections about the activity more vivid and accurate. This is especially important if you engage in an activity that takes several days to accomplish, such as climbing a mountain. As veteran writer, Tom Clynes says, "I travel with 'Rite-in-the-Rain' notebooks, which are an amazing invention, and write down only what I think will be relevant, so I don't get overwhelmed when I sit down to write."

Write the article in a narrative, first person essay style: Use "I" and insert yourself into the article. Unlike most forms of Journalism, participatory articles are primarily about you.

Use fiction techniques: Construct a central narrative, set scenes, present interesting characters, and tell the story in a compelling voice. Nonfiction has to live with the fact that real life isn't like a gripping thriller. You will need to decide what to leave out.

Impose yourself on the story: You need to make yourself a character in the story to get to the truth. There's no objectivity. Share your emotions with the reader, the ups and downs of the experience.

Describe your experience in detail: Describe the environment and the people around you. Include dialogue that you have with other people while you participate in the activity. Doing so makes the story come alive.

Use humour and self-deprecation: Express your fear and apprehension about participating in this new activity that you've never done before. These are good techniques to get the readers to relate to you. If you had a lump in your throat right before you were about to climb into a shark diving cage, your readers should have that lump as well as they read your description.

Say what you learned from participating in the experience: Give insight as to what it takes to do this activity. Would you want to do it again? Is it something you would encourage the reader to do? Mention what the readers should be aware of or look out for if they're going to participate in this activity, i.e. wear a helmet if you go snowboarding.

Shape your story: Remember that you have to add artistry to your experience. You should not write a chronological account of everything that you did. You need to forge a story line with a beginning, middle and an end.

Include telling details: You need to discern which details are relevant to move the story forward and cut the rest.

The autobiography essay

This is much more difficult and dangerous writing. By baring your past on the page you risk offending people. "Kill your parents." is the first thing I tell students in my journalism class. They all look a bit shocked, and interested, as most of them have actually considered killing their parents at some point. I explain that they cannot write well as long as parents, relatives or past lovers are breathing down their neck and censoring them.

Good advice, if you can follow it, I know. I have published only one first person autobiographical account in an article which I won't reproduce here.

TASK: Choose an activity that you've always wanted to do but never had an excuse. Use your imagination when choosing a topic. Now is the time to fulfil your lifetime dream to spend a day working as a used car salesman or estate agent. Now, find the drama in that activity. What part of your personality does it conflict with? Does second hand car dealing conflict with your inner honest Joe, for example?

Go have the experience. Write a first person account 800-1 000 words.

TASK: Experiment with your writing persona.

Rewrite your first person account, but adopt another persona. Read E. B. White and adopt his thoughtful persona in your account. Next read Dostoevsky's Underground Man. Adopt a ranting kind of persona in your first person account. Finally, read Joan Didion and rewrite your piece with mildly whining, self-deprecating humour.

TASK: Write a first person autobiographical essay, titled, *Something I wish I'd Never Done*. Preferably something that you've never told anyone. If you have no regrets, stop reading this book immediately and go out and get a life. Regrets are a writer's best friend. They make good copy.

Write on a piece of paper not a computer. Write about it in as much detail as possible, summoning the ghosts of your shame. When you've finished either burn the piece (you'll be glad you didn't use the computer!) or submit it for publication.

The human interest story

"I used to think I was the strangest person in the world but then I thought there are so many people in the world, there must be someone just like me who feels bizarre and flawed in the same ways I do. I would imagine her, and imagine that she must be out there thinking of me too. Well, I hope that if you are out there and read this and know that, yes, it's true I'm here, and I'm just as strange as you."

Frida Kahlo

Below are a few hints to help you write a compelling, emotionally appealing human interest feature:

Pick a topic which you like so that you can give it your best shot.

Focus on getting the emotion right.

What is it that you want your readers to feel at the end of the feature? Your aim is to create mood, emotion and atmosphere. Try to enable the reader to experience the emotion of the story: if it's sad, your reader should feel sad; if it's funny, your reader should laugh.

Use plenty of quotes.

If possible, let the person tell the story themselves with as little interruption as possible while still providing backstory and commentary so that readers can understand the context of their situation.

In many cases, an apt ending for both human interest stories and profiles is to give the central character the final say.

Write a nut graph

Put the subject of the story in context and show why the individual story matters.

Write an effective lede

The most suitable types of lede for human interest stories are anecdotal ledes that illustrate a certain quality that you want to emphasize about the person you are writing about. This is where you get your reader hooked into the story. Start with a short anecdote that's no longer than two paragraphs that shows, rather than telling, the point of your story.

Here's Anne Hulls powerful lede into Una Vida Mejora: A Better Life. Part 2 The Smell of Money

Delia Tovar tried to warn her younger sister about the smell.

It would linger on their skin, in defiance of lemon-water baths and rags doused with bleach. It would burn into the shine of their dark hair, inhabit their sheets and seep into their dreams.

Wandering the aisles of the Food-a-Rama, they would stink of crabs. Everyone would know they'd been brought from Mexico to do the work Americans refused.

"Think of it as the smell of money," Delia told her sister.

Human interest stories are often feel good stories designed to soften the blow of the "if it bleeds, it leads," rule. As humans we crave happy endings. However, the truth is often painful. For example, *The Jihadist next door*, by Andrea Elliot, published in The New York Times tells the extraordinary story of American Omar Hammami's evolution from a Southern raised, Baptist star student to spokesman for the Somalian guerrilla army, known as the Shahab.

Here is the chilling ending:

"I have become a Somali you could say." He writes in an email to his sister. "I hear bullets, I dodge mortars, I hear nasheeds (Islamic songs) and play soccer. Sometimes I live in the bush with camels, sometimes I live the five star life. Sometimes I walk for miles in the terrible heat with no water, sometimes I ride in extremely slick cars. Sometimes I'm chased by the enemy, sometimes I chase him!"

"I have hatred, I have love." He went on. "It's the best life on earth."

This ending brilliantly reflects the moral dilemma that Hammami and all extremist fanatics raise: how is it possible to do so much harm in the belief that you are doing right?

The profile feature

"I've learned that you can tell a lot about a person by the way he/she handles these three things: a rainy day, lost luggage, and tangled Christmas tree lights."

Maya Angelou

Meet the person you are profiling in their own environment

You learn most about a person by observing them in their everyday world, whether that's the football pitch or at the office. Let the sun, wind, rain and objects in the environment reveal your characters. When I was profiling Seth Rotherham, we arranged to meet at his local hangout, Caprice, a cocktail joint along Camps Bay beachfront which hosts Sunday night debaucheries. Seth arrived with what he called an angel in toe, wearing not much more than a pair of killer five inch heels. So far so bad boy. But half way through the interview, in a hilariously serendipitous moment, Seth's parents arrived and squeezed in alongside us, ruining the roguish image.

Show your character in action

As veteran writer Michael Lewis says, "Characters are always so much more interesting when they are moving through space than when they are at rest (especially when they are behind a desk in their office). Once I've developed a relationship with a subject, the first question I ask is whether they have plans to go anywhere, and whether I can come with them. Even when what they are doing is irrelevant to what I'm writing about, I just want to participate in something with them. ..I learned this technique in college, during the best job interview I ever had. I was applying for a job to lead a bunch of high school girls on a tour of Europe. When I arrived for the interview, the guy who was supposed to see me was flustered, and apologized. He said he was in the middle of moving his furniture from one office to another, and asked if I could help. So we spent the next hour moving his furniture together. It was brilliant on his part. The way he interviewed people was to make them do something with him. He believed he saw character more clearly that way. I agree."

Reveal your character's gifts

Readers are fascinated by people who excel in one field. We're not much interested in the mediocre, all-rounder. So when you research and write your profile focus on the one where your subject excels and forget the rest. That means work. If your character excels at tennis, you will need to become knowledgeable about tennis. You will need to watch him play. This doesn't mean that you have to know everything yourself, you can ask others to explain his genius. Think of master profile writer, Susan Orlean, who spent two years trailing around the South Florida swamps to explore the odd, passionate world of orchid fanatics for her book *The Orchid Thief*.

What physical traits make your character unique and admirable?

Most new writers think that telling readers about the colour of a characters hair, or what they wear, is creating character. They write bland sentences like "he had dark hair and wore jeans. She wore matching skirt and blouse." It's not. Physical description in and of itself is static and boring; it becomes more interesting when you use it to suggest, imply, and reveal character. Think about how your character's appearance impacts his/her life and personality. More telling questions are: Why does the character you are profiling dress like this? Are they comfortable in their clothes? Are the clothes they wear appropriate for the occasion?

Our appearance is our interface with the world. We shape and are shaped by it. If your character is unusually good-looking, for example, give some thought to the consequences of that.

Here's Jessica Pressler profiling Matthew McConaughey:

"McConaughey pointed to his famous pecs, peeking out of his white V-neck like a pair of toasted dinner rolls."

Capture your character's unique voice. Everyone has their own natural, signature way of talking.

Again in the McConaughey profile, "I saw Dallas Buyers Club, he says. "I liked it. I liked that guy. I didn't catch you acting, McConaughey, he said to himself afterward. "I forgot that was you, McConaughey." Addressing himself in the third person is a verbal idiosyncrasy which the author captures.

She goes on to quote him saying, "But it's an evolvement. It's a process." Leaving his usage of evolvement uncorrected.

Psychological profiling

A good profile probes. When you are reporting for your profile, go beneath the surface and ask:

What makes your subject complex?

What bad things have your good characters done and what good things have your bad characters done? Tomas Alex Tizon in his essay, *Every Profile is an Epic Story*, advises writers to remember that their subject is as complicated as they are. He writes, "It's very easy for journalists to create one-dimensional characters in their stories, especially when they consider only the person's official role as soldier, mayor, victim, and robber. To avoid that, I think about the mass of contradictions that I am and try to remember that others are too. This helps me guard against sentimentality and simplicity."

Each person has a dark side. Glimmers of that dark side give profiles their complexity.

Equally, people who commit evil acts have elements of kindness and compassion.

While not strictly a profile, Christopher Goffard's, *The Manhunt for Christopher Dorner* in the *Los Angeles Times* gives an account of an ex-police officer's nine-day killing spree in Southern California. At one point,

Dornier encounters an elderly couple who own the motel where he is hiding out. Here's what happens:

Dornier ordered them to lie face-down on the floor, then tightened zip-ties around their feet. Searching Jim's pockets, Dornier found a Hershey bar and asked if he was a diabetic.

"Yes," he said.

"Oh s---," Dornier said.

He put the chocolate between them on the carpet.

While clearly a psychologically damaged individual, the author chooses to show Dornier's capacity for kindness – not killing. By making him not wholly a monster has the effect of making the account even more chilling. Here is a killer who is capable of acts of compassion.

What's your subject's passion outside their area of expertise? Passionate people are interesting. They just are. They are dynamic and active; they care about something other than themselves. Even better if your character has an obsession. Obsession is interesting. It just is. An obsessed character wants something – or someone – in a way that creates drive, urgency, potential conflict, and story. An obsession also reveals a lot about character.

Who does your subject care about other than him or herself? As soon as you show the character genuinely caring about the world, the reader starts to care.

What's your subject's psychic wound? The past is alive in all of us. The past has trained us to react in certain ways. If your character was used or shamed as a child, that's going to affect him as an adult: he might seek solace in a fantasy world, he might fear intimacy and pursue novelty and intensity instead. Stuff like that.

The more you know about your character's past, the more you know about how your character reacts to the present.

What is your subject's attitude? How does he or she relate to other people? No one lives in a vacuum. Does your subject think she's inferior or superior? Is she trusting, or mistrustful? Is she introverted or attention-seeking?

How does your character treat people, and how do people treat your character in return?

What does your subject want the most at this stage of his life? Desire rules us. We go after the things that we want.

What does your subject fear the most? How has he confronted his fears? What fear is your character now confronting in order to get what he wants.

What are your subject's blind spots? There are things we know about ourselves, and that other people know about. Then, there are things we know about ourselves that other people don't know about. Every profiler wants their subject to reveal secrets about themselves. But remember, actions speak louder than words. I'm constantly amazed in my everyday interactions by the pronouncements that people make about themselves:

"I'm a very tidy person," my messy friend tells me. "I'm very generous," a stingy person says. People have idealized opinions of themselves. When writing a profile and someone makes such a statement, ask them to give evidence. What is the most generous thing you have ever done? How much do you give to charity? How much do you pay your workers?

How do others view your subject? A good profile interviews widely around a subject. Their parents, best friend, arch enemy, seeking to show the various facets that make up any character. Gay Talese claims that he interviewed "At least a hundred" people for his Sinatra profile.

There are things other people can see and know about us that we actually don't know about. Interestingly, it's often the most accomplished people who hold the lowliest opinions of themselves. Even generally confident people can be surprisingly insecure about their particular gift.

The gap between self-perception, and the perception of others, can lead to some interesting observations in your profile.

The interview

The interview is an essential part of writing the profile, although Sinatra refused an interview with Gay Talese who, in 1966, went on to write one of the most famous profile features, *Frank Sinatra has a Cold*. However, the interview has its limitations. People do not always see themselves clearly. Each and every one of us has a blind spot, part of our personality about which we are oblivious and which is glaringly obvious to others. In interviews, people may be either self-effacing or self-aggrandizing. So while the interview can yield valuable information, it isn't the final say about a person. What can be more interesting is the tension between what people say about themselves and what others say about them.

Even if time does not permit you to interview other people, you can still pick up contradictions between what people say and how they interact with their environment. For example, health fanatics fascinatingly contradictory creatures. Many refuse to eat anything other than organic vegetables while happily smoking up a storm.

In an excoriating Rolling Stone profile about famous self-help author Scott Peck, the author noticed the gaping contradiction between Pecks claim that love required discipline and the author's inability to defer any gratification. While his book preached that "delaying gratification is the only decent way to live," he smoked, drank heavily, and let his children roll joints for him because they enjoyed his sometimes oppressive company more when he was stoned. "Children who are truly loved . . . unconsciously know themselves to be valued. This knowledge is worth more than any gold," he waxed in his writing, but his funeral notice cold-bloodedly announced he was survived by two children, not three, since one of his daughters disowned him.

So, remember, don't take the people that you are interviewing at their word, probe.

Another famous profile, *The Duke of His Domain*, was penned by Truman Capote and published in the November 9, 1957. Capote met with Brando in Kyoto, Japan, where he was filming *Sayonara*, and spent several hours drinking and conversing in Brando's hotel.

Capote told the editor of the New Yorker that he wanted to take the "very lowest form of journalism," that is, the celebrity profile, and transform it into a "new genre." He would apply "the technique of fiction, which moves both horizontally and vertically at the same time: horizontally on the narrative side and vertically by entering inside its characters."

Truman lets Brando's diet reveal his undisciplined and overindulgent character:

"I'm supposed to be on a diet. But the only things I want to eat are apple pie and stuff like that." Six weeks earlier, in California, Logan had told him he must trim off ten pounds for his role in *Sayonara*, and before arriving in Kyoto he had managed to get rid of seven. Since reaching Japan, however, abetted not only by American-type apple pie but by the Japanese cuisine, with its delicious emphasis on the sweetened, the starchy, the fried, he'd regained, then doubled this poundage. Now, loosening his belt still more and thoughtfully massaging his midriff, he scanned the menu, which offered, in English, a wide choice of Western-style dishes, and, after reminding himself "I've got to lose weight," ordered soup, beefsteak with French-fried potatoes, three supplementary vegetables, a side dish of spaghetti, rolls and butter, a bottle of sake, salad, and cheese and crackers.

Structure of the profile

The lede:

Profile features often kicks off with an anecdotal lede, like the profile of the Palaeontologist, quoted earlier.

Capote uses the dramatic lede in his Brando interview:

 The little maid on the fourth floor of the Miyako Hotel, in Kyoto, led me through a labyrinth of corridors, promising, "I knock you Marron." The "l" sound does not exist in Japanese, and by "Marron" she meant Marlon - Marlon Brando, the American actor, who was at that time in Kyoto doing location work for the motion picture version of James Michener's novel *Sayonara*.

"Oh, hi," he said. "It's seven, huh?" We'd made a seven o'clock date for dinner; I was nearly 20 minutes late. "Well, take off your shoes and come on in. I'm just finishing up here." Looking after the girl as she scurried off, he cocked his hands on his hips and, grinning, declared, "They really kill me. The kids, too. Don't you think they're wonderful, don't you love them - Japanese kids?"

The body:

The profile should be broken into paragraphs that each explore an aspect of the person you are profiling. Keep each paragraph focused on a distinct idea. Think of each paragraph as a scene in a movie. Keep the setting the same and work with the same characters in one paragraph. Don't, for example, mix biography and physical description.

Action: Show the person being profiled in action. Let his actions speak louder than words.

Here's Gay Talese dramatizes Sinatra's temper:

Frank Sinatra, leaning against the stool, sniffling a bit from his cold, could not take his eyes off the Game Warden boots. Once, after gazing at them for a few moments, he turned away; but now he was focused on them again. The owner of the boots, who was just standing in them watching the pool game, was named Harlan Ellison, a writer who had just completed work on a screenplay, *The Oscar*.

Finally Sinatra could not contain himself.

"Hey," he yelled in his slightly harsh voice that still had a soft, sharp edge. "Those Italian boots?"

"No," Ellison said.

"Spanish?"

"No."

"Are they English boots?"

"Look, I donno, man," Ellison shot back, frowning at Sinatra, then turning away again.

Now the poolroom was suddenly silent. Leo Durocher who had been poised behind his cue stick and was bent low just froze in that position for a second. Nobody moved. Then Sinatra moved away from the stool and walked with that slow, arrogant swagger of his toward Ellison, the hard tap of Sinatra's shoes the only sound in the room. Then, looking down at Ellison with a slightly raised eyebrow and a tricky little smile, Sinatra asked: "You expecting a storm?"

Harlan Ellison moved a step to the side. "Look, is there any reason why you're talking to me?"

"I don't like the way you're dressed," Sinatra said.

"Hate to shake you up," Ellison said, "but I dress to suit myself."

Now there was some rumbling in the room, and somebody said, "Com'on, Harlan, let's get out of here," and Leo Durocher made his pool shot and said, "Yeah, com'on."

But Ellison stood his ground.

Sinatra said, "What do you do?"

"I'm a plumber," Ellison said.

"No, no, he's not," another young man quickly yelled from across the table. "He wrote *The Oscar*."

"Oh, yeah," Sinatra said, "well I've seen it, and it's a piece of crap."

"That's strange," Ellison said, "because they haven't even released it yet."

"Well, I've seen it," Sinatra repeated, "and it's a piece of crap."

Now Brad Dexter, very anxious, very big opposite the small figure of Ellison, said, "Com'on, kid, I don't want you in this room."

"Hey," Sinatra interrupted Dexter, "can't you see I'm talking to this guy?"

Dexter was confused. Then his whole attitude changed, and his voice went soft and he said to Ellison, almost with a plea, "Why do you persist in tormenting me?"

The whole scene was becoming ridiculous, and it seemed that Sinatra was only half-serious, perhaps just reacting out of sheer boredom or inner despair; at any rate, after a few more exchanges Harlan Ellison left the room. By this time the word had gotten out to those on the dance floor about the Sinatra-Ellison exchange, and somebody went to look for the manager of the club. But somebody else said that the manager had already heard about it — and had quickly gone out the door, hopped in his car and drove home. So the assistant manager went into the poolroom.

Even better than what others say is others reactions. Later, in one succinct sentence, Talese captures perfectly the reaction of others to Sinatra:

When he strolled into the studio the musicians all picked up their instruments and stiffened in their seats.

Lyn Barber uses a telling detail to show Marianne Faithfull's cool hippy passivity through her inaction:

I first glimpsed Her Fabulousness ages ago at a restaurant in Notting Hill, 192, where she was sitting all alone at lunchtime reading the papers. 192 is a very sociable sort of table-hopping restaurant, so I thought there was something faintly sad about her solitude. But then a man joined her - it might even have been my future nemesis, François - and she simply handed him a slice of newspaper and carried on reading right through lunch. It was so devastatingly drop-dead cool that all the chattering at the other tables somehow died.

The ending

One convention in profile writing is letting the person profiled have the last word. Here's how Truman Capote ends his interview with Marlon Brando:

The telephone's racket seemed to rouse him from a daze. He walked me to the door. "Well, sayonara," he mockingly bade me. "Tell them at the desk to get you a taxi." Then, as I walked down the corridor, he called, "And listen! Don't pay too much attention to what I say. I don't always feel the same way."

The ending cleverly mocks the convention of the profile, questioning whether readers should bother paying attention to what celebrities say when they are being interviewed.

Some writers hold that the journalist is the expert and should have the last word. Having the last word is a power play. Here's Lyn Barber getting her own back at Marianne Faithfull and demonstrating Susan Sontag's dictum that writing well is the best revenge. This is also a terrific example of a well-structured profile, with the ending, or kicker linking back to the lede and hence bringing the story full circle.

Here's the lede:

Marianne Faithfull once said, 'I am a Fabulous Beast, and as such, I should only be glimpsed very rarely, through the forest, running away for dear life.' How wise she was. If I were ever asked to interview her again, I would turn into a Fabulous Beast myself and hightail it to the forest. I first glimpsed Her Fabulousness ages ago at a restaurant in Notting Hill, 192, where she was sitting all alone at lunchtime reading the papers. 192 is a very sociable sort of table-hopping restaurant, so I thought there was something faintly sad about her solitude. But then a man joined her - it might even have been my future nemesis, François - and she simply handed him a slice of newspaper and carried on reading right through lunch. It was so devastatingly drop-dead cool that all the chattering at the other tables somehow died - we farmyard animals knew we were in the presence of a Fabulous Beast.

And the ending:

Oh, she is exasperating! She is so likeable in some ways but also such a pain. The question that was spinning round my head the whole time was: Who does she think she is? She is a singer with one good album (*Broken English*) to her credit, an actress with one or two good films. Really, her main claim to fame is that she was Mick Jagger's girlfriend in the 60s, but of course she would never admit that. She thinks she's a great artist who has yet to unleash her full genius on the world. Maybe one day she will, and then I will beg to interview her again on bended knee. Till then, back to the forest, you tiresome old Fabulous Beast.

Lyn Barber nearly always has the last word; it's part of her signature style. Here she is being generous to Christopher Hitchens.

Right at the end of *Letters to a Young Contrarian*, Hitchens confesses to 'a slight sense of imposture' and quotes James Cameron, saying that every time he sat at his typewriter he thought, 'Today is the day they are going to find me out.' Find him out as what, though? What is the imposture? Believe me, I was looking for it - some chink between words and actions that I could burrow into and say, "Aha!" But, actually, the more I looked, the more impressed I was by his sincerity. He does plough quite a lonely furrow; he does keep banging on about thankless subjects like Cyprus or

Northern Ireland; he does make frequent and dangerous trips to uncomfortable countries, not just newsworthy war zones, but nasty, dreary hell-holes like North Korea. It's true he writes for money - for *Vanity Fair* - but he also writes for no-hoper leftie reviews and small publishers simply because he wants to get the stuff out.

Perhaps his sense of imposture is the one all writers have - that they care more about writing than they do about their subject. This is something non-writers can never imagine, because they always think of writing as a chore. But Hitchens is never happier than when writing: 'Some people feel that they have to write - it's not a choice, or a preference, it's a determination. I've been very lucky - that's the thing I can't get over - that I can make my living from doing the only thing I like and the only thing I can do. Writing is recreational for me, I'm unhappy when I'm not doing it.' A pleasure for him, then, and a pleasure for his readers. If that's his idea of imposture, I think we can forgive him.

Narrative ending:

Here's how Talese ends his epic Sinatra profile:

THE REST OF THE MONTH was bright and balmy. The record session had gone magnificently, the film was finished, the television shows were out of the way, and now Sinatra was in his Ghia driving out to his office to begin coordinating his latest projects. He had an engagement at The Sands, a new spy film called *The Naked Runner* to be shot in England, and a couple more albums to do in the immediate months ahead. And within a week he would be fifty years old….

Life is a beautiful thing

As long as I hold the string

I'd be a silly so-and-so

If I should ever let go...

Frank Sinatra stopped his car. The light was red. Pedestrians passed quickly across his windshield but, as usual, one did not. It was a girl in her twenties. She remained at the curb staring at him. Through the corner of his left eye he could see her, and he knew, because it happens almost every day, that she was thinking, It looks like him, but is it?

Just before the light turned green, Sinatra turned toward her, looked directly into her eyes waiting for the reaction he knew would come. It came and he smiled. She smiled and he was gone.

The travel feature

"Travel writing is one of the oldest forms of our craft. The story of going to a strange place and then returning home is an archetype going back at least to Homer's Odyssey, written (or spoken) some 2,800 years ago. In this form the author tells of a geographical journey that parallels an inner journey – from illusion to understanding, from ignorance to knowledge."

Adam Hochschild *Telling True Stories*

Much of what passes for travel writing in magazines and websites is perhaps more aptly described as vacation writing: an article that lists the pleasures of visiting a popular tourist destination that is often driven more by commercial concerns – such as the willingness of the publication to give an advertiser more exposure – than interest for the reader.

The best travel writing ignores the obvious. Or if the writer undertakes to write about the pyramids at Gaza, or the Eiffel tower in Paris, does so with an anthropologist's objectivity or a philosopher's detachment. For example, David Foster Wallace's *Shipping Out*, written after a week-long cruise. Even before the cruise departs, the adverts insistence on having fun induces cynicism and melancholy in the writer:

"The promise is not that you can experience great pleasure but that you will. They'll make certain of it. They'll micromanage every iota of every pleasure-option so that not even the dreadful corrosive action of your adult consciousness and agency and dread can fuck up your fun. Your troublesome capacities for choice, error, regret, dissatisfaction, and despair will be removed from the equation. You will be able – finally, for once – to relax, the ads promise, because you will have no choice."

Whilst the best topics for travel features are the unusual or the undiscovered, this doesn't mean that you are restricted to writing about expensive, exotic locations. Good travel features ask the reader to look more closely at familiar places. The best travel writing invites us to enter unfamiliar worlds but the alien and unusual is easily found a few streets, blocks or miles away.

And what is it that a travel feature attempts do? Like any feature, a good travel feature has a clear narrative arc. You often want to avoid writing that reads like a series of visual snapshots.

The obvious narrative arc for a travel story is leaving and returning home. But don't start your story with the hour long delay at the airport and end when the wheels of your plane hit the tarmac. In *My London, and Welcome to,* AA Gill imagines the reader perusing his feature before landing in Heathrow:

"If you've saved this article for your long-planned trip to London, and you're now reading it for the third time, circling Heathrow, well, I'm sorry. You're probably still up there because the queue at passport control has become mutinous. They're snaking out onto the runways — grim, silently furious visitors, unable to use their phones, forbidden from showing anything but abject acquiescence to the blunt instrument that is the immigration officer at the distant desk."

Often the best narrative arc for travel features, as Adam Hochschild suggests in *Telling True Stories*, outlines the writer's inner journey from incomprehension to clarity. Like a photographer adjusting the focus of his lens, gradually a city, or country, comes into sharper focus as the writer realizes the core qualities that make the place distinctive.

Consider, again, *My London, and Welcome to It:*

"London is a city of ghosts; you feel them here. Not just of people, but eras. The ghost of empire, or the blitz, the plague, the smoky ghost of the Great Fire that gave us Christopher Wren's churches and ushered in the Georgian city. London can see the dead, and hugs them close. If New York is a wise guy, Paris a coquette, Rome a gigolo and Berlin a wicked uncle, then London is an old lady who mutters and has the second sight. She is slightly deaf, and doesn't suffer fools gladly."

In *City of Djinns: A Year in Delhi*, William Dalrymple gradually comes to realize that partition - when the British Indian Empire was dissolved and the territory segmented into India and Pakistan - underlies almost everything that he encounters in Delhi:

"Even the most innocuous of our neighbours, we discovered, had extraordinary tales of 1947: chartered accountants could tell tales of single-handedly fighting off baying mobs; men from grey government ministries would emerge as the heroes of bloody street battles."

People and places are inextricably intertwined. Can you imagine Paris populated by Americans or Japanese? It would be an entirely different city. When you are writing about a place, let your writing come alive through the people who live there. Quotes from local characters can bring your writing to life, give the locals a voice and make a point it would take longer to explain yourself.

As a travel writer you have permission to eavesdrop.

A A Gill tells us more about London with this snippet of overheard dialogue than any number of scenic descriptions:

"On the bus recently a middle-aged, middle-class, middleweight woman peered out of the window at the stalled traffic and furiously bellowed; "Oh my God, is there no end to these improvements?" It was the authentic voice of London, and I thought it could be the city's motto, uttered at any point in its history, embroidered in gold braid on the uniforms of every petty official."

The best travel writing is fresh and creative; the worst is laden with clichéd phrases. If you are attempting to write about place, you need to choose your words with particular care. As Zinsser warns in *On Writing Well* "Nowhere else in nonfiction do writers use such syrupy words and groaning platitudes. Adjectives you would squirm to use in conversation – "wondrous," "dappled," "roseate," "fabled," "scudding" – are common currency. Half the sights seen in a days' sightseeing are quaint, especially windmills and covered bridges: they are certified for quaintness. Towns situated in hills (or foothills) are nestled – I hardly ever read about an unnestled town in the hills – and the countryside is dotted with byways, preferably half forgotten."

Avoid platitudes. No travel writer should ever be excused for describing a place as rich in history. Frankly, which place isn't? Nor, for the same reason, should you ever tell your readers that a place offers "Something for everyone."

Avoid Subjectivity: What do words like characterful or beautiful mean? Everyone has their own individual idea of what is beautiful and full of character. One good tip is to describe things as if you were explaining them to a blind person.

Avoid hyperbole: Using words like "stunning," "incredible," "awesome" and "breath-taking," are the linguistic equivalent of waving your arms and jumping up and down.

Similarly with superlatives: Unless you're being intentionally subjective, use the word best with care. Unless you can factually verify it, use the words "largest" and biggest with caution.

So, skip the majestic mountains, golden beaches and bustling markets and instead use detailed description. Describe the outer landscape as clearly and accurately as possible, as though you are describing it to a blind person.

Travel writing nudges against the memoir genre as the writer is a character in his own adventure. So think about how you want to relate to your readers. Do you want to come across as a learned authority, an expert dispensing knowledge, like Peter Ackroyd in *London: The Biography*? Or do you prefer a warmer approach that invites the reader to accompany you on a journey of discovery, like Dalrymple in *City of Djinns: A Year in Delhi*.

Don't be afraid to include your thoughts, perceptions and feelings about a place. Some of the best travel writing is about the effects that a place has on us, how we are changed by a place. For Mark Salzman, who taught English in China, a "bleak or beautiful" landscape means nothing "until a person walks into it, and then what interests me is how a person behaves in that place."

Don't even attempt to write a definitive, objective account of a place. As veteran travel writer Jan Morris says, "The nature of my writing is that I write about myself, really. All the books I've ever written are terribly egotistical and self-indulgent. People sometimes say, 'You've been to Paris,' for example, 'and it wasn't a bit like I found it'. Well, of course it wasn't how you found it, you oaf, I was writing about it not you! I wasn't writing about how it affected you, I was writing about how it affected me."

"The future will be determined in part by happenings that it is impossible to foresee; it will also be influenced by trends that are now existent and observable."

Emily Greene Balch

The trend feature

To find the latest trends you'll need to do some old-fashioned reporting. Go online and check out what people are talking about on social networking sites. Visit a local college campus to see what's up. The object is to track down whatever it is that's generating a buzz at the moment.

Here are some tips for writing trend stories:

Make sure its current

A good trend writer has their finger on the pulse of contemporary life and culture. Trend stories should focus on what's new. There's nothing worse than a trend story that's out of date. So when you're fishing for ideas for trend pieces, make sure they're fresh. Example: A story about the Facebook craze would have been fresh in 2004 or 2005. Now it's old news.

Keep it light

Trend stories are generally meant to be light reading. So write them that way. Unless you're dealing with a serious topic (sexting among teens might be an example), set seriousness aside and make your story one people will want to read.

Keep it concise

A trend story should be on the short side. Keep it tight, light and bright.

Keep it real

Journalists are sometimes derided for writing stories about trends that, well, aren't really trends. So make sure whatever you're writing about is real and not the figment of someone's imagination or something only a handful of people are doing.

Analyse the trend

Where does the story lie? What are the causes or consequences of the trend? Regardless of where you choose to focus the story, you must keep the readers aware of where this trend lies in the chain of cause and effect. In short, tell them what is causing the trend and make sure they are aware of what the possible implications might be.

Use specific examples that demonstrate how and why this trend is occurring.

Generally, there are two ways to handle trend features: through focusing intensely on one person or situation that illustrates the situation, or through a broad-brush sampling of many individual cases. As a general rule, the best material comes from those with the closest exposure to the trend.

Give an expert overview of the subject area.

Besides individuals directly affected by or involved with the subject, you will need to interview someone with an overview, a neutral expert who is knowledgeable about the subject.

"The perfect ending should take your readers slightly by surprise and yet seem exactly right. They didn't expect the article to end so soon, or so abruptly, or say what it did. But they know it when they see it. Like a good lead, it works."

Too often students, schooled in essay writing style end their features with a summary, basically repeating what they have said in the rest of the feature. This won't do."

William Zinsser, *On Writing Well*

THE ENDING

Here are some professional ways to round off your feature

Circle back to the lede.

A brilliant example of this is Lyn Barber's interview with Marianne Faithfull, quoted earlier.

End with a quotation.

Read through your notes and find a remark that has some sense of finality, or adds a telling detail.

I used in this in a profile about self-styled playboy, Seth Rotherham:

"So with a new five-star residence in Green Point, has the playboy of the Atlantic Seaboard turned his back on Camps Bay? 'Not at all,' Seth insists. 'Camps Bay's got everything: sex, money, fast cars, beaches, sunsets. I am Camps Bay.'"

Truman Capote uses it to brilliant effect in the end of his interview with Marlon Brando.

The telephone's racket seemed to rouse him from a daze. He walked me to the door. "Well, sayonara," he mockingly bade me. "Tell them at the desk to get you a taxi." Then, as I walked down the corridor, he called, "And listen! Don't pay too much attention to what I say. I don't always feel the same way."

Another way to end a feature is to look ahead. This is how Gene Weingarten ends his heart-breaking feature, Fatal Distraction, about parents who have forgot a child in the back seat of a hot, parked car.

"Can you imagine losing your only child and not having a hope of having another? Can you imagine that despair?"

That's why, she says, she's made a decision. She's checked it out, and it would be legal. There would be no way for any authority to stop it because it would fall into the class of a private adoption. She'd need a sperm donor and an egg donor, because she wouldn't want to use her own egg. That would make it too personal.

What is she saying, exactly?

Miles and Carol Harrison deserve another child, Balfour explains measuredly. They would be wonderful parents.

This is the woman you either like or don't like, right away. She is brassy and strong-willed and, depending on your viewpoint, refreshingly open or abrasively forward. Above all, she is decisive.

Balfour says she's made up her mind. If Miles and Carol Harrison are denied another adoption, if they exhaust all their options and are still without a baby, she will offer to carry one for them, as a gift.

A final word of encouragement...

"The thing about writers is that, with very few exceptions, they grow slowly—very slowly. A John Updike comes along, he's an anomaly. That's no model, that's a phenomenon. I sent stuff to *The New Yorker* when I was in college and then for ten years thereafter before they accepted something. I used to paper my wall with their rejection slips. And they were not making a mistake. Writers develop slowly. That's what I want to say to you: don't look at my career through the wrong end of a telescope. This is terribly important to me as a teacher of writers, of kids who want to write."

John Mcphee

Printed in Great Britain
by Amazon